buckeyes

buckeyes

THE LEGENDARY CANDY
OF THE MIDWEST

Cyle Young

RED ⚡ LIGHTNING BOOKS

This book is a publication of

Red Lightning Books
1320 East 10th Street
Bloomington, Indiana 47405 USA

redlightningbooks.com

Manufactured in the United States of America

ISBN 978-1-68435-023-0 (cloth)
ISBN 978-1-68435-025-4 (ebook)

First printing 2021

contents

preface

I'm a Buckeye—not by choice, but by birth. Born in Ohio, I'm a Buckeye through and through. In my heart, I bleed maize and blue. Yes, that means I crossed the northern border to play football at the University of Michigan. But once a Buckeye, always a Buckeye—I just don't like the state's most famous football team.

Buckeye candies have been a part of my life for as long as I can remember. The chocolate peanut butter balls were one of my favorite desserts growing up—but there were never enough. No one ever showed up at a dinner party with dozens of buckeyes; each tray or bowl would only have around ten to twenty buckeyes. I would always claim dibs and stock my plate with five or six before receiving a disapproving look from someone much older than myself.

Now, as an adult, I can make as many buckeyes as I want. I also realize why no one takes large numbers of buckeyes to a party. They either hoard the delicious little nuggets for themselves, eat most of the buckeyes at home before the party, or realize how much work it takes and only share a small portion. In my experience, I have found all three reasons to be accurate.

Using this book, you can make loads of buckeyes at your leisure. Play around with the recipes and try all sorts of new buckeye candy–inspired drinks, cakes, and desserts. You don't have to hoard them for yourself like I do—but they're so delicious, no one could blame you if you did.

One of my favorite moments at the University of Michigan took place because of the buckeye candy. Every year, the training staff would bring in hundreds of buckeye candies to help the team prepare for playing the Ohio State Buckeyes on Saturday. My teammates and I would devour those buckeyes, just as we hoped to do to our opponents during the game. We didn't always win the game, but every time I got to eat buckeyes was a personal victory for me.

Your buckeye experience will be different than mine, but I hope that inside these pages, you'll learn about the history of the buckeye tree and how it inspired the famous candy, discover how the buckeye nut helped a president win the highest office in the land, and acquire the knowledge to make some fantastic buckeye dishes and desserts.

acknowledgments

I thank Grandma and Grandpa Eubanks for their love of family and friends. Each New Year's Eve, my grandparents hosted the all-night party that forever sealed my love for the famous buckeye candy. As a small boy, I reveled in the delicious treat and raided candy and cookie platters for the chocolatey, peanut-buttery balls. They never lasted long, but each year ended with another taste of buckeye candy, and each new year brought a longing for more.

I also appreciate the names I've since forgotten of all the wonderful people who brought the candy platters to those parties decades ago. Without you, this book would never have materialized.

To my mom, thanks for all the times you made buckeyes. They weren't your favorite dessert to make, and now as an adult I know why. They aren't the easiest or fastest candies to make.

To Kellie Brockway, thanks for helping me make *hundreds* of buckeyes in Youngstown, Ohio. Your mother's recipe is one of my favorites—of course, I've never met a buckeye candy I didn't like.

buckeyes

1

The Buckeye Candy

The buckeye candy is Ohio's native candy. The delicious dessert perfectly resembles its namesake, the nut from the buckeye tree—Ohio's state tree. Never eat an actual buckeye— they're slightly poisonous. But you should never avoid the delicious buckeye candy. Millions of Ohioans have been enjoying this delicacy since somewhere in the mid-1970s.

The trees grow all across the state, and Ohioans love their buckeyes. The Buckeye State is home to the third-largest public university in the United States. Situated in the state capital of Columbus, Ohio, the Ohio State University is home to the Buckeyes. Ohio State fans cheer on their favorite teams with *lucky* buckeye necklaces on, and you'll often find the university's famous O logo emblazoned with a buckeye leaf and buckeye nut. Even more homage is given to the famous plant, as the university's football team features Brutus the Buckeye as the mascot at every game. It's safe to say that Ohio, and more particularly its centralized capital, is the center of Buckeye Nation.

No true Ohioan and no Ohio State fan will ever be found far from the famous buckeye candy. Every fall, little round balls of sweet, peanut-buttery goodness are rolled and dipped in chocolate to resemble the buckeye nut. Platters of buckeyes appear at fan tailgates, at church potlucks, at family gatherings, and on cash register displays. And it only takes one small bite of a buckeye to get hooked for life.

Stores all across Ohio have cashed in on the buckeye craze, and now buckeye candies can be shipped all over the United

States and abroad to satiate the cravings of former Ohioans living in the diaspora. If you want to give a special gift to those who have ever called Ohio home, send them a dozen buckeyes in the mail. Not only will they appreciate the sweet sentiment and delicious candy, your gift will transport them back to many fond memories of growing up and enjoying life in the heart of the Midwest—the Buckeye State.

The buckeye candy has grown in popularity over the years, partly because of the success of the university's football team bringing attention to the Buckeyes and partly because Ohioans have moved outside the state and have continued to share the love of their native candy with the outside world. People who have never tried a buckeye compare their first bite to Reese's Peanut Butter Cups. The tastes are similar, but the presentation of a buckeye makes all the difference. A perfect buckeye candy resembles a buckeye nut—a piece of home and a part of tradition—and no other candy can replicate that.

2

History of the Buckeye Tree

The buckeye candy is based upon the nut of the Ohio state tree, *Aesculus glabra*, more commonly known as the Ohio buckeye or American buckeye. This species of tree is also often referred to as the horse chestnut. The nuts of the tree are poisonous and should never be eaten, which makes this an unusual tree to inspire a look-alike candy. But the oblong brown seed with its unique light-brown basal scar has become synonymous with both the state of Ohio and the university that bears its namesake, the Ohio State Buckeyes.

The Ohio buckeye tree has leaves that expand like palm fronds into five distinct leaflets. It grows in southwestern Ontario, throughout the Midwest, and as far south as the Nashville, Tennessee.

What's in a Name?

The name *buckeye* became associated with the tree during the early pioneer days. In spring 1788, Captain Daniel Davis is said to have cut down the first tree west of the Ohio River. He coined the name *buckeye tree*, and the designation has stood to this day. The term *buckeye* came from local Indians who would use the word *hetuck* in admiration of early settlers who'd impressed them. The Indian word literally meant "the eye of the buck deer." The term could also mean "big buckeye," which was fitting for the tall Colonel Ebenezer Sproat, the first recorded settler nicknamed Hetuck. Sproat founded the city of Marietta, Ohio. Over time, *buckeye* would come to be used as the colloquial word to describe people who lived in the Ohio territory and later the state of Ohio.

Largest Tree

The largest Ohio buckeye tree in the state of Ohio stands in Huron County. The seventy-seven-foot tree held the crown as the nation's largest buckeye until the discovery of a larger Ohio buckeye in Oak Brook, Illinois. The new champion sits on the campus of McDonald's corporate headquarters and is more than 150 years old. The Oak Brook buckeye tree is actually four feet shorter than its Ohio cousin, but due to its larger girth around the trunk and impressive canopy, the Illinois tree outscores the Huron County tree.

3

People, Places, and Things (and the Buckeye Candy)

Even though the buckeye candy tradition only dates back to 1964, it has left a lasting impression on the state of Ohio and its citizens. Dozens of chocolate and confectionary businesses have sprung up across the state to feed the insatiable hunger for the state's namesake candy. Hundreds of thousands of pounds of buckeyes are handmade every year across the Buckeye State. The buckeye craze manifests itself in unique ways, and it has been part of Ohio lore for more than 250 years.

Calvin and Hobbes

Bill Watterson is one of Ohio's most famous cartoonists. The comic strip artist is best known for *Calvin and Hobbes*. It is believed that Watterson's hometown of Chagrin Falls, Ohio, served as the inspiration for the strip's setting. In the comic, Calvin often uses buckeye nuts to torment Hobbes or flirt with his neighbor, Susie Derkins.

Buckeye Tool

Making buckeye candies in massive batches takes loads of time, especially when you have to hand dip each buckeye. At Winans Chocolates + Coffees in Piqua, Ohio, they solved this dilemma with the invention of a special tool—the buckeye tool. Dixon Clement, a shop teacher at the local high school, came up with the nifty invention to help speed the production of hand-dipped buckeye candy. Dixon's invention combines copper and brass into a three-pronged buckeye dipper. The tool resembles a large fork with a transverse sliding bar that releases the chocolate-coated buckeyes. During a facility tour, you can see both the three-pronged and five-pronged versions of the buckeye tool.

Buckeye Tradition

The buckeye candy tradition dates back to 1964. Fourteen years after the Ohio State University declared its new school mascot, Gail Lucas invented the unique dessert. Interestingly enough, Gail did not herself attend Ohio State; she was an alumnus of Marshall College in West Virginia. In 1964, she lived in Columbus, Ohio, and worked at the *Citizen-Journal*. Her husband, Steve, was a rabid buckeye fan who was also pursuing his PhD in business at Ohio State.

Leather Tanning

Native Americans used the indigenous plant to assist in the leather tanning process. Blanched buckeye nuts released tannic acid, which they used to tan leather. In more modern times, the buckeye nuts have been turned into charms and jewelry. Dried buckeyes darken and turn hard when they are left exposed to air for a period of time. They can then be strung into necklaces or bracelets much like pearls or kukui nuts.

Largest Buckeye Candy

Marsha's Homemade Buckeyes in Perrysburg, Ohio, holds the world record as creator of the world's largest piece of buckeye candy. The 339-pound buckeye candy consisted of 75 pounds of peanut butter, 75 pounds of margarine, 10 pounds of chocolate, and 150 pounds of powdered sugar. The record buckeye candy made its appearance at the 2018 Ohio State Fair and unseated the previous record holder, a 271-pound buckeye made by Coco Beans Candy Cupcakes and More in Fremont, Ohio.

Big Nut

Fremont, Ohio, resident Jon Peters is known as the Big Nut. Peters is the Ohio State University's self-proclaimed biggest fan. During the 2002 Football National Championship Game in Tempe, Arizona, Peters dressed up for the school's pep rally. He painted his face gray on one side and scarlet on the other. He placed two massive strings of buckeyes around his neck and adorned himself with a helmet resembling one worn by the team. His final adornment was a replica jersey with his nickname on the back, Big Nut.

The Big Nut has become an Ohio celebrity. He regularly receives invitations to celebrity events and is booked for appearances across the state. The Big Nut has sealed a place in Ohio Buckeye lore, and if you are paying close attention, the television camera almost always pans to him during every Ohio State home football game.

Presidential Nut

During the 1880 presidential election, future president William Henry Harrison used the buckeye nut as a symbol for his campaign. Harrison not only adopted the visage of the nut, he commonly wore buckeye necklaces at his speaking engagements. His supporters fashioned the nuts into crude buttons, built log cabins out of buckeye wood and hauled them in wagons to political rallies and parades, and carved buckeye wood canes to support their blue-collar candidate. Harrison's political strategy would not only win him the election but forever seal Ohio as the Buckeye State.

Marbles

First published in 1889, T. F. Thiselton-Dyer's book *The Folk-lore of Plants* shares some amusing insights on buckeyes in chapter 18:

> A Worcestershire name for a horse-chestnut is the "oblionker tree." According to a correspondent of *Notes and Queries* (5th Ser. x. 177), in the autumn, when the chestnuts are falling from their trunks, boys thread them on string and play a "cob-nut" game with them. When the striker is taking aim, and preparing for a shot at his adversary's nut, he says:—
> "Oblionker!

My first conker (conquer),"
the word oblionker apparently being a meaningless
invention to rhyme with the word conquer, which has by
degrees become applied to the fruit itself.[1]

Midwestern boys used to play a version of marbles, "a 'cob-nut game,'" using buckeyes instead of marbles. *Oblionker* might sound like the name of a spell out of a Harry Potter book, but it shows the creativity with which nineteenth-century boys used to come up with a rhyming word for *conquer*. Thiselton-Dyer's books also shows that the tradition of wearing buckeyes as neck-laces has been going on for a long time in the Midwest.

Half-Poisonous?

Some people believe that only half of the buckeye nut is poison-ous, but humans can't figure out which. Only squirrels know which half of each buckeye nut is poisonous and which half is not. This belief explains why some squirrels will eat buckeye nuts and the remnants of half-eaten nuts are strewn all about the Midwest. Yes, adherents of this view would have to believe that squirrels are smarter than humans—at least not the one that ran in front of my car last week.

Lucky Nut

Many superstitions surround the buckeye nut. Throughout recorded history are instances of the buckeye nut being treated as a lucky horseshoe or rabbit's foot. Here are some ways to carry your buckeye charm:

- Carried in your pocket, a buckeye brings good luck.
- Carried in your pocket, a buckeye brings you money.
- Three buckeyes carried in your pocket will help you always to have money.
- A buckeye stored in your purse, carried on yourself, or left in your house brings good luck.
- A buckeye carried in your right pocket will bring you good luck during a card game or a baseball game.

Sexual Prowess

Gerina Dunwich shares in her book *Herbal Magick* that "buckeye nuts are believed by some hoodoo 'doctors' to increase a man's sexual power. Shaped like miniature testicles, they are sometimes carried in the pants pockets as charms to bring men 'good fortune in sexual matters.'"[2] So there you have it: some believe buckeyes are a natural treatment or remedy for infertility and erectile dysfunction. I wouldn't bet on it, but it sure is a humorous belief.

Health Nut

The buckeye nut goes well beyond just being a gambling charm. In buckeye folklore, the nut has been able to cure and prevent many ailments. From rheumatism and infertility, the buckeye nut is like having a doctor in your pocket. Here's a list of a few of the ailments a buckeye nut is said to prevent or cure:

- A buckeye carried in the right pocket will cure rheumatism and hemorrhoids or piles.
- A buckeye carried in your pocket will prevent chills all year long.
- A buckeye carried in your pocket prevents you from getting sick.
- A person who carries a buckeye in his pocket will never have a backache or headache.
- If you are really sick, you should carry buckeyes in pairs. If you do, the buckeyes will also make you lucky.

Be careful: losing a nut while curing or preventing sickness is said to bring very bad luck. You don't want the bad luck that comes from losing a buckeye nut, so best to hang on to your nuts. And never eat a buckeye. For one, we know they are poisonous. And two, superstition says that if you eat a buckeye, your head will turn around.

4

The "Original" Buckeye Recipe

The buckeye candy tradition dates back to 1965, fourteen years after the Ohio State University declared its new school mascot, Gail Lucas invented the unique dessert. Interestingly, Gail did not herself attend Ohio State. She was an alumnus of Marshall College in West Virginia. In 1964, she lived in Columbus, Ohio, and worked at the *Citizen-Journal*. Her husband, Steve, was a rabid Buckeye fan who was pursuing his PhD in business at Ohio State.

The invention of the buckeye candy was merely a sweet coincidence. Gail's mother had previously sent her some chocolate-covered peanut butter candy. Her family loved the candies so much, Gail asked her mother to share the recipe with her. During Christmas 1964, Gail replicated the recipe, but when she used a toothpick to dip a peanut butter ball into the chocolate, she realized it looked familiar. It looked exactly like a buckeye.

Needless to say, the happy accident would also please her Buckeye husband. That day, the buckeye candy was born. Gail made multiple batches of the candy and gave them away to family and friends. But she didn't share her mother's recipe until her husband graduated from the university in 1971.

Steve's new career required the family to move away from Columbus. A family friend repeatedly asked Gail to share her buckeye candy recipe. Gail eventually relented and gave in to the pestering. But during a return visit to Columbus in 1973, Gail discovered a newspaper article about her buckeye candy. She'd go on to discover that same woman had written to the *Ohio State Alumni Magazine* and claimed to be the inventor of the recipe.

Gail had been betrayed. She was furious. For well over a decade, she and her family had celebrated the buckeye candy tradition, especially during the Ohio State–Michigan rivalry weekend. In a 1983 column in the *Arizona Republic* newspaper, Gail set the record straight: we have her to thank for the delicious buckeye candy that lives on during every football season in Ohio.

In 2012, Gail finally joined the great confectionary in the clouds. Her son, Guy Lucas, a second-generation journalist, found his mother's 1983 column when he was going through her belongings. He decided to share it with the world so everyone would know the true inventor of the buckeye candy. Now you too can enjoy the original Buckeye Balls.

Gail Lucas's Buckeye Balls

Ingredients:

4 pounds powdered sugar
1 pound butter
6 or more tablespoons peanut butter
2 teaspoons vanilla
12 ounces chocolate chips
1 block canning wax

Directions:

Combine first four ingredients, adding a bit of milk if necessary. Roll into small balls. Melt chocolate chips and canning wax in top of double boiler. Make sure chocolate and wax are mixed well so wax doesn't rise to the top. With toothpick, dip the balls into the chocolate, but do not cover completely. Chill in refrigerator. After chocolate is hardened, store candy in plastic bags in freezer.[1]

Over the last sixty years, while the buckeye has grown in popularity, its history has come into question. Who is the real creator that launched a midwestern craze and turned this amazing dessert into a delicacy? Although the history of the buckeye candy is clouded, there is one uniting factor that every maker of buckeye candy can agree upon—the ingredients.

Powdered Sugar

Heaping mounds of powdered sugar turn the mess of ingredients into a perfectly round ball of dough. The more the better. Every buckeye recipe calls for different amounts of powdered sugar, but one thing remains the same—it's always the main ingredient on the list. You can skimp on the powdered sugar, but you risk losing flavor and turning the sweet delicacy into a ball of bland mush.

When you are ready to make buckeye candies, stock up on as much powdered sugar as you can store. You will use it. It's not uncommon to use more than five pounds of powdered sugar to make a large batch. If you want to make enough to last the season, you could need as much as ten to fifteen pounds.

Butter or Margarine?

The choice between butter and margarine is highly debated. Which tastes better in a buckeye? I guess it depends on which one you prefer in your everyday routine. Do you butter your toast or put margarine on it? I would say that whatever you use on toast is the correct answer for which to use in your recipe. If you're really adventurous, replace some of the butter with lard. You may shorten your life a little, but your buckeyes will be insanely delicious.

Whichever fat you decide to use, just make sure to follow the recipe. I have used both butter and margarine, and I can't really tell a difference between the two—but if you are a butter snob, use the best butter you can find. The fat helps to hold all the ingredients together, as buckeyes are a no-bake dessert.

Peanut Butter

The decision on which peanut butter you use for your buckeye candies may be the most important one you make. Whatever you do, don't use natural peanut butter. The oil separates too easily and will ruin your buckeyes. You'll find yourself staring at an oily, misshapen pile of goo if you don't use the right kind of peanut butter. Natural is healthier for sure, but if you are eating true buckeye candies, you aren't really worried about your health, are you? You can be adventurous and use crunchy peanut butter. It won't hurt your flavor, and the added crunch will add a little bit of texture to your buckeyes.

Chocolate

Everybody loves chocolate. I think that the chocolate you choose is the second-most important decision you make for your buckeye candy. Semisweet chocolate seems to be the most popular choice of most buckeye candymakers, but adding a unique chocolate can brighten the flavors, heighten the enjoyment, and tease the palate.

Dark chocolate adds a bitterness that can be a nice change from the sweetness of the powdered sugar. White chocolate adds a silkiness to the texture but steers away from the traditional look of the buckeye—it doesn't resemble the nut much at all. Still, using white chocolate allows you to add food coloring. Changing the color of the chocolate lets you play around with the buckeye candy, and if you aren't a fan of the Ohio State University, you can make buckeyes in your favorite team's colors: green and white for Ohio University; red and white for Miami of Ohio; black and red for University of Cincinnati; yellow (or gold) and blue for Toledo, Akron, and Kent State; orange and brown for Bowling Green State University; and, of course, maize and blue for the team up north—the University of Michigan.

Play around with the chocolate and find the ones you like best. Part of the fun of the buckeye candy is creating a unique version that is an extension of your personality and creativity in the kitchen.

Wax

Most buckeye candy recipes call for paraffin wax. Paraffin helps the chocolate melt without congealing in the heat. It also helps the buckeye candy hold its glossy shine once it has cooled. The amount of paraffin differs among cooks and varies among recipes. You can use as little or as much as you prefer.

Thanks to new regulations in some states, paraffin wax has a cancer warning on the box. This comes from the health and beauty industry. Breathing a significant amount of aerosolized paraffin can lead to nausea or lung cancer.[2] This is not a risk in cooking, but it is if you make a living giving manicures and pedicures. The National Library of Medicine has deemed that paraffin is safe to eat in small quantities,[3] for example, in buckeye candies. The only risk in cooking with paraffin is in eating enough that it clogs up your bowels. People cannot digest paraffin, so it passes right through the digestive tract. Unless you are eating hundreds of buckeyes in one sitting, you'll be fine. Bakers have been using paraffin for decades with no problem. Chefs and candymakers across the globe use it in moderation.

If you are worried about using paraffin, though, you can try one of the alternatives on the market. The natural alternative is beeswax. But beeswax comes with a mild change in flavor and shouldn't be used or consumed by persons with a bee allergy. The most commonly used substitute is almond bark. Almond bark is a misnomer: it doesn't contain almonds and is safe for people with nut allergies. It is made up of sugar, partially hydrogenated vegetable oil, milk, and artificial coloring and flavors. If you don't have any almond bark lying around, you can use vegetable oil to help melt the chocolate, although you will lose the added bonus of wax helping to hold the buckeye's form.

Vanilla

Not every buckeye candy recipe calls for vanilla. The choice to use it is purely a preference. If you decide to add vanilla to your batch of buckeye dough, make sure to get a high-quality vanilla. Don't settle for imitation; splurge on the real stuff. If you don't have access to real vanilla, you can make it. Purchase a cheap bottle of 80-proof vodka, and insert a half-dozen split vanilla bean pods into it. The brand of vodka doesn't matter—the cheaper the better. Make sure it doesn't have any added flavor.

Vanilla Extract (at home)

Ingredients

Grade B Madagascar bourbon vanilla beans—5 per
8 ounces of vodka (Any vanilla beans will do. If you can't
get grade B, just double the amount in the recipe.)
Bottle of vodka, 80 proof (neutral flavor)

Directions:

1. Cut vanilla beans in half lengthwise and scrape out the flecks inside. Don't discard the flecks—you will need them.

2. Add the split vanilla beans and the discarded flecks to the bottle of vodka. You may have to pour a little vodka out to make room for the beans.

3. Seal the bottle and place it in a cool, dark place. The vanilla will ripen, but it takes time. Allow for at least eight weeks before use. Be aware the flavor gets better with age. If you can wait six months to a year before use, you won't be disappointed.

Tips for Melting Chocolate

Perfectly melted chocolate is necessary to make the buckeye candy. Learning to properly melt the sweetest and most decadent chocolates will send your buckeye candy recipes to new heights. Many of the recipes in this book require melted chocolate, either for dipping or drizzling. Melting chocolate is never as simple as it seems, and these tips and tricks will help you melt chocolate like a pro.

Melting Tips

Dry all your tools: One drop of water can cause you to lose an entire batch of melted chocolate. Dry off your bowl, your whisk, and whatever kitchen instrument you use to store the chocolate. Any moisture can cause your chocolate to seize up. Seized chocolate turns into a gritty, clumpy blob. Properly melted chocolate should be runny and smooth.

When water interacts with the sugar in the chocolate, it turns into a liquid syrup. The remaining cocoa particles begin to clump with the loss of the sugar, and the once smooth chocolate turns dry and large lumps form.

Seized chocolate can be rescued. You'll need to let it cool and then restart the melting process. This time proceed more slowly. You will need to add heavy cream a little at a time and whisk the mixture until smooth. This reactivated chocolate will be noticeably less flavorful than before, but it should still work well for chocolate drizzle over strawberries, brownies, or ice cream.

Go slow: The number one problem most people have with melting chocolate is increasing the heat too fast and not properly tempering the chocolate. Tempering chocolate is the process of heating and cooling that helps to stabilize the chocolate for use in creating candies and confections like the buckeye. Remember: slow and steady wins the race. When you cook chocolate low and slow with even heat, you will create the perfect melted chocolate every time. When you raise the temperature too fast, chocolate will become grainy. And if the temperature becomes too high, you will burn the chocolate. There is no saving the chocolate once it is burned.

Make sure that you stir the chocolate while you are melting it. The edges of your melting bowl are usually the coolest. By stirring the center of your melted chocolate to the edges, you create even heat dispersion, which will enable the perfect Goldilocks zone for your chocolate—not too hot and not too cold.

Use smaller pieces: A rookie mistake in chocolate melting is using pieces of chocolate that are too big. Roughly chop your chocolate into smaller pieces to allow the heat to disperse evenly over the chocolate surface faster. Smaller chocolate pieces have more surface area, allowing the heat to do its work faster. Make sure those pieces are cut close to the same size; consistently sized pieces allow the chocolate to melt evenly and will protect your bowl of chocolate from getting burned.

Buy higher-quality chocolate: If you buy cheap chocolate, you are going to get what you pay for. All chocolate is delicious, but not all chocolate is equal. Not all chocolate melts the same either. Melted chocolate with a silky, smooth finish starts with purchasing the right quality or brand of chocolate. Look for words like *candy-melting chocolate*, *Dutch chocolate*, or *melting chocolate* on the package. You can also look at the ingredients; chocolate with a higher cocoa butter content will be better for melting.

Chocolate chips work in a pinch, but since they were designed to survive in an oven, they aren't your best choice for fancy buckeye candies. If you are making a small batch, feel free to try out melting different brands of chocolate chips. When you want to create impressive buckeye desserts, look for the word *couverture*. Couverture chocolates have a minimum of 31 percent cocoa butter and are specifically designed to be used as a coating. They are easy to temper and are perfect for even a novice baker to use. You may not find them at your local grocery store, but you'll be able to find them at most specialty groceries or online. Look for brands like Cacao Barry, Scharffen Berger, Valrhona, and Callebaut.

Use a candy thermometer: Chocolate hates to go above 130 degrees. It is best melted between 110 and 115 degrees Fahrenheit. A candy thermometer will help you check the temperature of your chocolate to ensure it doesn't increase to a level that will scorch or burn it.

The best temperature for coating, drizzling, or dipping buckeyes is around 87–100 degrees Fahrenheit, depending on your specific type or brand of chocolate. Many good-quality chocolates will list the best melting and molding temperatures on their packaging.

Chocolate-Melting Methods

There are many different ways to skin a cat, and there are many different methods to melt chocolate. These six ways below will help make you a confectionary specialist—at least in your own kitchen. If you have struggled melting chocolate in the past, try some of the different methods to discover what works best for you. The fastest way isn't always the best, and with higher-quality chocolate, you may have to use more involved chocolate-melting methods.

Microwave Method

The microwave is the easiest and fastest way to melt chocolate—when it works. Because each brand of microwave is so different from other brands, there isn't a standard set of melting instructions. Some microwaves can be set at 70 percent power. In those microwaves, you can heat the chocolate for one minute before stirring and then in thirty-second increments thereafter.

Other microwaves don't have a power setting. In those microwaves, you place the chocolate in a microwave-safe dish and heat on high for thirty seconds. After thirty seconds, stir the chocolate and return it to the microwave for another thirty-second blast. Remove and stir and repeat this process until the chocolate is fully melted.

The microwave melting method isn't the most scientific option, but if you need a quick fix of melted chocolate, it'll do the trick. I prefer the microwave for quick drizzling or small batches of buckeyes or buckeye bark.

Water Bath Method

You will need a slow cooker for this method. You'll also want some wide-mouth mason jars or some other deep glassware dish. Depending on the size of your slow cooker, fill it one-third to one-half full with hot water. The water level should be high enough to cover the height of your chocolate in the mason jars.

Fill mason jars with chopped or grated chocolate. You can fill each mason jar with a different type of chocolate if you are making a recipe that calls for more than one. Place the mason jars in the water. Be sure not to let any water get into the chocolate or you will have a seized-up chocolate mess.

Set the slow cooker on high and a timer to thirty minutes. When the timer goes off, you should have some ready to dip or drizzle melted chocolate. If it's not quite melted, stir the chocolate, wait another five to ten minutes, and you'll be good to go.

This is a great chocolate-melting method to use with children in the kitchen. If you want them to have the fun of making buckeyes without the chance of getting burned, this is the melting method for you.

Double Boiler Method

Don't own a double boiler? Don't worry—most people don't. You can purchase a double boiler at most stores, but you can also just place a metal or glass bowl over a pot to make a homemade version. Make sure your bowl is bigger than the rim of the pot.

Fill the pot with water and place it on the stove over medium heat. It's important that the water simmers but doesn't reach a boil. If the water boils, the steam will be too hot, which will cause your chocolate to become dry and clumpy. Also, make sure that the bottom of your bowl is higher than the water. If the water touches the bowl, the chocolate will get too hot and burn or scorch.

Place your chocolate in the metal or glass bowl. Stir gently and constantly until all the chocolate has completely melted. I have found that a rubber spatula helps to scrape and incorporate all the chocolate from the sides of the bowl.

Sandwich Bag Method

You can use this method to dip buckeyes, but it will be very messy. The sandwich bag method is better saved for when you are melting chocolate to drizzle or decorate.

You will need a resealable sandwich bag. Place chopped or grated chocolate in the bag. Make sure you get a tight seal on the bag. If you are concerned about water seepage, you can place the sandwich bag inside an additional bag for more protection. Once the chocolate is sealed in the sandwich bag, place it in a bowl of hot water. Ensure the water is not boiling. Chocolate melts around 110–115 degrees Fahrenheit, so water just hot enough that you can't stand to touch it with your bare hand should be adequate.

Allow the chocolate to melt completely. Once removed from the water, you can smoosh the chocolate around a bit with your fingers to ensure all the pieces have melted. Using scissors, cut a small hole in the corner of the bag just large enough to form the perfect-size bead of drizzle. Squeeze the bag to force the chocolate through the hole to drizzle or decorate your dish.

Direct Heat Method

You can melt chocolate in a pan on the stove over direct heat. This method is not recommended for dipping buckeyes, but it can be useful for some chocolate-melting applications.

To melt over direct heat, you must add your chocolate to a fat like vegetable oil, batter, margarine, or butter. Place your chosen fat in a saucepan with the chocolate on very low heat, and stir constantly. If the heat is too high or you don't stir it enough, your chocolate will scorch. When only a few clumps of unmelted chocolate remain, remove the pan from the heat and stir until all the chocolate has melted completely. You will need to use the melted chocolate quickly because it will begin to cool and set away from the heat.

Selecting the Best Peanut Butter for Making Buckeyes

Every buckeye recipe requires two things—chocolate and peanut butter. I've spent a good deal of time discussing the best chocolate and melting techniques, but what about choosing the right peanut butter for making buckeyes? Your selection of peanut butter does make a difference, and the kind of peanut butter you use will affect your recipe. With so many options at your grocery store—natural, gluten-free, low fat, sugar-free, etc.—how do you know what to pick?

Natural or Name Brand?

The biggest decision you will need to make when making buckeye candy is what kind of peanut butter you will use. The type of peanut butter you choose can and will impact the overall taste of your dessert. I don't suggest choosing a natural type of peanut butter because the oils tend to easily separate at room temperature and natural peanut butter may give your buckeye batter a thinner, runnier feel, which will not allow your buckeye balls to bind together properly.

Name-brand peanut butter like Jif and Peter Pan has fillers and additives that help the peanut butter stay perfectly emulsified and smooth, even at room temperature. These types of peanut butter are better for baking, as they maintain the same consistency in recipe after recipe. I recommend taste-testing store brands to find your favorite and then using that in your buckeye recipes. If your heart's set on using natural peanut butter, you will have to increase your baking time in recipes where some elements are baked to allow for the extra moisture from the oils, and you will have to add some fillers or extra powdered sugar in buckeye candy recipes that don't require baking.

Health Conscious?

Every recipe that uses some form of health-conscious peanut butter substitute will require trial and error to discover exactly how the substitute affects each recipe. Almond, sunflower, and cashew butter are similar to natural peanut butter as substitutes—they all tend to be runnier alternatives to store-bought peanut butter—but they can add variety to your recipes and help you cut back on unhealthy additives.

Hummus and tahini paste can be used to substitute for peanut butter. Both hummus and tahini paste have unique flavor profiles that will change the way your buckeye dessert tastes. These ingredients have a creamier, more liquid consistency and may require additives to any recipes they are used in.

Chunky or Smooth?

Once you have determined the type or peanut butter you are going to use, your next decision is whether to use chunky or smooth. This decision is important to the overall consistency of your buckeye dish. Whether you choose chunky or smooth peanut butter is more up to your palate and what kind of texture you want your recipe to have. My suggestion is to vary the texture of your dishes to add a little variety and spice things up every once in a while.

5

Recipes

Buckeye Candy Recipes

Today, buckeyes come in all shapes, flavors, and sizes. There is a buckeye for every palate or diet. Try some of these recipes until you find the perfect buckeye candy for you. And don't worry if you can't eat peanuts or are living a low-carb lifestyle—we've got recipes for those too. Get ready to start baking this one-of-a-kind candy, and you don't even have to be from the state of Ohio to enjoy this delicious dessert.

Disclaimer: Please remember to drink responsibly for any recipes that contain alcohol, and be assured you can always use a nonalcoholic substitute.

Who would have ever thought of mixing potato chips with buckeyes? Someone did, and the mixture of salt and sweet will send your taste buds on a journey of delicious discovery. This recipe can be crafted as stated below, or you can substitute the white chocolate for dark chocolate or milk chocolate for more taste sensations. Mixing in different types of potato chips also opens this recipe up to a world of taste possibilities.

Potato Chip White Chocolate Buckeyes[1]

Ingredients

1 cup creamy peanut butter
6 tablespoons butter, at room temperature

½ cup powdered sugar

1 teaspoon vanilla

2 cups finely crushed rippled potato chips, divided

16 ounces white chocolate almond bark, broken into pieces

Directions

1. Combine peanut butter and butter. Mix until smooth.

2. Add powdered sugar gradually until well combined.

3. Fold in vanilla and then mix in 2 cups potato chips until fully incorporated.

4. Roll dough into roughly 1-inch balls and place on a pan lined with parchment paper.

5. Place in the freezer for 15–20 minutes.

6. Melt the chocolate using a double boiler or saucepan while the doughballs are cooling.

7. Pick up the doughballs with a toothpick and then dip the balls, one at a time, into the melted chocolate. Leave an exposed circle to resemble the spot of the buckeye.

8. Return the chocolate-coated balls to the parchment-lined pan and sprinkle with remaining potato chips.

9. Place in refrigerator for 5 minutes to set the chocolate.

Who doesn't love a little bourbon in their buckeyes? Try one of these delicious nuggets and take a little edge off. Bourbon Buckeyes make a great addition to any cocktail party. These alcohol-infused treats also make a great tailgate snack for any Ohio State football fan. Of course, you can still take them to your next football game even if you are rooting against the Buckeyes. Who said they can keep this delicious candy all to themselves?

Bourbon Buckeyes[2]

Ingredients

1 ½ cups creamy peanut butter
1 cup butter, softened
1 teaspoon vanilla
1 teaspoon kosher salt
5 cups powdered sugar
¼ cup bourbon
1 cup toasted pecans
3 cups dark chocolate chips
⅛ cup coconut oil

Directions

1. Combine softened butter, salt, vanilla, and creamy peanut butter until fully incorporated.

2. Add powdered sugar gradually until well combined.

3. Fold in bourbon.

4. Roll dough into roughly 1-inch balls.

5. Press a pecan into a doughball and then roll the ball around in your hand to incorporate the pecan into the doughball.

6. Place rolled balls on a pan lined with parchment paper and place in the freezer for 15–20 minutes.

7. While the balls are in the freezer, melt dark chocolate chips and coconut oil in a double boiler.

8. Using toothpicks, pick up the peanut butter balls and dip them into the melted chocolate. Be careful not to dip the entire ball; leave a small uncovered area to make the buckeye.

9. Place the chocolate-covered balls back onto the wax paper and then return to refrigerator until chocolate is firm and set.

The traditional buckeye candy is not the best dessert for the most health conscious of midwestern citizens. But don't fret; I have the perfect healthy buckeye recipe for you, and it even packs a decent protein punch to help you stave off sugary cravings. You can use your preferred sugar substitute, but the recipe calls for stevia. Cashew or macadamia nut milk can be substituted in this recipe to tweak the flavor profile.

Healthy Buckeye Balls[3]

Ingredients

1 cup unflavored protein powder
¾ cup peanut flour
½ teaspoon salt
1 ½ cups unsweetened vanilla almond milk
½ cup natural peanut butter
1 ½ teaspoons liquid stevia
1 teaspoon vanilla
½ cup 70 percent cacao dark chocolate
1–2 tablespoons coconut oil

Directions

1. Combine protein powder, peanut flour, salt, vanilla, stevia, and peanut butter until fully incorporated.

2. Mix in almond milk.

3. Roll dough into roughly 1-inch balls.

4. Place rolled balls on a pan lined with parchment paper and place in the freezer for 15–20 minutes.

5. While the balls are in the freezer, melt dark chocolate chips and coconut oil in a double boiler.

6. Using toothpicks, pick up the buckeye balls and dip them into the melted chocolate. Be careful not to dip the entire ball; leave a small uncovered area to make the buckeye.

7. Place the chocolate-covered balls back onto the parchment paper and refrigerate until chocolate is firm.

Allergic to peanut butter? No worries. This recipe for Almond Butter Buckeyes will allow you to enjoy the buckeye candy without fear. You can substitute almond butter in any of the buckeye recipes, but this unique recipe adds cinnamon and salt to help highlight the almond substitute. Cashews, walnuts, or pecans could be used instead of almonds. Each nut will change the flavor characteristics, and you may decide to increase or decrease the xylitol for taste.

Almond Butter Buckeyes[4]

Ingredients

½ cup butter, softened
¾ cup almond butter
1 teaspoon vanilla
Pinch of Himalayan salt
½ teaspoon Ceylon cinnamon
½ cup xylitol
½ cup coconut oil
¼ cup cacao powder
⅛ teaspoon stevia (more or less to taste)

Directions

1. Combine butter, almond butter, vanilla, one pinch of salt, and cinnamon until fully incorporated.

2. Add xylitol gradually until well combined.

3. Roll dough into roughly 1-inch balls.

4. Place rolled balls on a pan lined with parchment paper and place in the freezer for 15–20 minutes.

5. While the balls are in the freezer, melt cacao powder and coconut oil together in a double boiler. Mix in stevia to taste.

6. Using toothpicks, pick up the almond butter balls and dip them into the melted chocolate. Be careful not to dip the entire ball; leave a small uncovered area to make the buckeye.

7. Place the chocolate-covered balls back onto the parchment paper and refrigerate until chocolate is firm.

Buckeye candy without the carbs. The keto trend is storming the nation, and this recipe allows keto adherents to enjoy this delicious snack. It's worth noting that once you add up all the net carbs, you will probably only be able to eat one Keto Buckeye each day. But one Keto Buckeye is always better than none. Serve these candies at your next health-conscious party; they will for sure be a hit with the crowd.

Keto Buckeyes[5]

Ingredients

1 cup peanut butter or almond butter
1 ¼ cups almond flour
¼ cup powdered erythritol
1 cup sugar-free chocolate chips

Directions

1. Combine peanut butter, almond flour, and powdered erythritol until well combined.

2. Roll dough into roughly 1-inch balls.

3. Place rolled balls on a pan lined with parchment paper and place in the freezer for 15–20 minutes.

4. While the balls are in the freezer, melt chocolate chips in a double boiler.

5. Using toothpicks, pick up the peanut butter balls and dip them into the melted chocolate. Be careful not to dip the entire ball; leave a small uncovered area to make the buckeye.

6. Place the chocolate-covered balls back onto the parchment paper and refrigerate until chocolate is firm.

Paleolithic humans never ate buckeye candies, but they should have. Paleo Buckeyes allow you to use only the ingredients of a paleolithic diet to concoct an almond-buttery treat to break up the monotony of sweet potatoes, salad, and almond flour. You can substitute honey for the maple syrup or coconut flour for the almond flour if you prefer. Make these at your next paleo party for a unique change of pace.

Paleo Buckeyes[6]

Ingredients

½ cup almond butter
¼ cup coconut butter
⅓ cup almond flour
2 tablespoons maple syrup
1 teaspoon vanilla
½ 10-ounce bag Enjoy Life chocolate chips
1–2 tablespoons coconut oil

Directions

1. Melt the coconut butter over low heat.

2. Combine coconut butter, almond butter, almond flour, vanilla, and maple syrup until fully incorporated.

3. Roll dough into roughly 1-inch balls.

4. Place rolled balls on a pan lined with parchment paper and place in the freezer for 15–20 minutes.

5. While the balls are in the freezer, melt chocolate chips in a double boiler.

6. Add coconut oil to chocolate to get desired consistency.

7. Using toothpicks, pick up the almond butter balls and dip them into the melted chocolate. Be careful not to dip

the entire ball; leave a small uncovered area to make the buckeye.

8. Place the chocolate-covered balls back onto the parchment paper and refrigerate until chocolate is firm.

Diabetic-accessible buckeyes are no longer just a dream. These Sugar-Free Buckeyes will have low impact on your blood sugar levels. Before you mix these buckeye balls, carefully check the ingredients to ensure that you are using all low-sugar and no-sugar options to craft these sugar-free nuggets of goodness.

Sugar-Free Buckeyes[7]

Ingredients

1 cup peanut butter (no sugar added)
½ cup butter, softened
½ cup Swerve Confectioners sweetener
½ cup vanilla protein powder
1 teaspoon vanilla
1 teaspoon vanilla liquid stevia
1 cup dark chocolate (85 percent Lindt)
2 tablespoons butter (for chocolate)

Directions

1. Combine peanut butter, butter, vanilla, stevia, and protein powder until fully incorporated.

2. Mix in Swerve until well combined.

3. Roll dough into roughly 1-inch balls.

4. Place rolled balls on a pan lined with parchment paper and place in the freezer for 15–20 minutes.

5. While the balls are in the freezer, melt chocolate and butter in a double boiler.

6. Using toothpicks, pick up the peanut butter balls and dip them into the melted chocolate. Be careful not to dip

the entire ball; leave a small uncovered area to make the buckeye.

7. Place the chocolate-covered balls back onto the parchment paper and refrigerate until chocolate is firm.

You may not even know what popped quinoa is, but it is delicious in buckeye candy. The ancient grain gives the buckeye a special crunch and taste like a mix between a Nestlé Crunch bar and a buckeye ball. Try to purchase the quinoa already popped. If you have to pop the quinoa yourself, the recipe can take much longer and will require more preparation and cleanup. You can find popped quinoa at some health-conscious grocery stores.

Popped Quinoa Buckeyes[8]

Ingredients

10 Medjool dates, pitted
¼ cup creamy peanut butter
½ teaspoon vanilla
¼ cup popped white quinoa
1–2 tablespoons water, if needed
2 ounces semisweet chocolate
1 teaspoon coconut oil
Sea salt (garnish)

Directions

1. Place dates in a food processor and pulse until they are in small pieces. Melt the coconut butter over low heat.

2. Add peanut butter and vanilla. Pulse until fully incorporated.

3. Add popped quinoa and pulse a few times until well mixed. Add a tablespoon of water, one at a time, until dough is desired consistency.

4. Roll dough into roughly 1-inch balls.

5. Place rolled balls on a pan lined with parchment paper and place in the freezer for 15–20 minutes.

6. While the balls are in the freezer, melt chocolate chips in a double boiler.

7. Add coconut oil to chocolate to get desired consistency.

8. Using toothpicks, pick up the peanut butter balls and dip them into the melted chocolate. Be careful not to dip the entire ball; leave a small uncovered area to make the buckeye.

9. Sprinkle finished buckeyes with sea salt.

10. Place the chocolate-covered balls back onto the parchment paper and refrigerate until chocolate is firm.

If you don't know what cookie butter is, you are missing out. This recipe substitutes cookie butter for peanut butter, and the result is a delicacy for any true cookie lover. A normal buckeye mixes salt and sweet together, but Cookie Butter Buckeyes are engineered just for your sweet tooth. These buckeyes are perfect accoutrements to any midwestern birthday party celebration.

Cookie Butter Buckeyes[9]

Ingredients

½ cup creamy cookie butter
3 tablespoons unsalted butter, softened
1 cup powdered sugar
1 teaspoon vanilla
½ cup semisweet chocolate chips
¼ teaspoon coconut oil

Directions

1. Combine cookie butter, butter, powdered sugar, and vanilla until fully incorporated.

2. Roll dough into roughly 1-inch balls.

3. Place rolled balls on a pan lined with parchment paper and place in the freezer for 15–20 minutes.

4. While the balls are in the freezer, melt chocolate chips in a double boiler.

5. Add coconut oil to chocolate to get desired consistency.

6. Using toothpicks, pick up the cookie butter balls and dip them into the melted chocolate. Be careful not to dip the entire ball; leave a small uncovered area to make the buckeye.

7. Place the chocolate-covered balls back onto the parchment paper and refrigerate until chocolate is firm.

I always think of Starbucks when I think of cake pops. The coffee store sells some for over two dollars each. You won't have to spend nearly that much to make your own Buckeye Cake Pops at home. This recipe is time-consuming, but the end result is worth it. When you combine peanut butter cake, peanut butter frosting, and chocolate, how could it go wrong?

Buckeye Cake Pops[10]

Ingredients

PEANUT BUTTER SHEET CAKE

2 cups all-purpose flour

2 teaspoons baking powder

½ teaspoon salt

¾ cup creamy peanut butter

¾ cup unsalted butter, softened

1 ½ cups sugar

2 large eggs

1 teaspoon vanilla

¾ cup whole milk

PEANUT BUTTER FROSTING

½ cup unsalted butter, softened

½ cup creamy peanut butter

½ teaspoon vanilla

Pinch of salt

1 ¾ cups powdered sugar

1 tablespoon heavy cream

FOR COATING

24 ounces dark chocolate candy chocolate, chopped

½ cup peanut butter (garnish)

Lollipop sticks

Directions

PEANUT BUTTER SHEET CAKE

1. Preheat the oven to 350 degrees Fahrenheit.

2. Line a cake pan with parchment paper.

3. Mix flour, baking powder, and salt.

4. In a separate bowl, combine butter, sugar, and peanut butter until smooth.

5. Add eggs, one at a time, to the peanut butter bowl, stirring each time, and then add the vanilla.

6. In a series of alternating pours, stir in flour mixture and milk into the peanut butter mixture.

7. Pour batter into the cake pan and bake for 30 minutes or until toothpick comes out clean.

8. Let cool completely before handling.

PEANUT BUTTER FROSTING

1. Mix butter, peanut butter, salt, and vanilla until thoroughly combined.

2. Slowly add the powdered sugar until incorporated.

3. Add heavy cream and beat until smooth.

To make the cake pops

1. Crumble cake into a large bowl.

2. Add ¼ cup peanut butter frosting and mix until mixture sticks together. Continue adding peanut butter frosting ¼ cup at a time until mixture can be formed into a ball.

3. Roll mixture into roughly 1-inch balls.

4. Place rolled balls on a pan lined with parchment paper and chill in refrigerator for 2 hours.

5. While the balls are in the fridge, melt chocolate in a double boiler.

6. Using lollipop sticks, pick up the cake balls and dip them into the melted chocolate until fully covered.

7. Place the lollipop sticks in a stand or Styrofoam to allow excess chocolate to drip off.

8. Refrigerate until chocolate is firm.

10. Melt peanut butter and drizzle across the top.

11. Chill until ready to serve.

Don't let bourbon have all the fun. You can use Kahlúa to make buckeye candies for your next tailgate or event. The addition of crunchy peanut butter raises the saltiness to new heights and cuts through the Kahlúa flavor with each crunch. Choose your favorite name brand of crunchy peanut butter for this recipe. As you know, choosy moms choose Jif, but Peter Pan and Skippy will always work too.

Crunchy Kahlúa Buckeyes[11]

Ingredients

½ cup crunchy peanut butter
3 tablespoons unsalted butter, melted
1 teaspoon vanilla
1 cup powdered sugar
¼ teaspoon salt
¼ cup Kahlúa
1 cup semisweet chocolate chips
1 tablespoon unsalted butter
1 tablespoon milk
Handful of sea salt

Directions

1. Combine peanut butter, melted butter, powdered sugar, vanilla, powdered sugar, and salt until fully incorporated.

2. Roll dough into roughly 1-inch balls.

3. Place rolled balls on a pan lined with parchment paper and place in the freezer for 15–20 minutes.

4. While the balls are in the freezer, melt chocolate chips in a double boiler.

5. Add the butter and Kahlúa to chocolate to get desired consistency.

6. Using toothpicks, pick up the peanut butter balls and dip them into the melted chocolate. Be careful not to dip the entire ball; leave a small uncovered area to make the buckeye.

7. Place the chocolate-covered balls back onto the parchment paper and refrigerate until chocolate is firm.

8. Sprinkle cooling buckeyes with sea salt.

This recipe is perfect for winter. Every time I think of gingerbread, I think of mounds of midwestern snow and ice on the ground outside. Grab a cup of peppermint mocha and sit by the fire nibbling on these gingerbread snacks. You may equate gingerbread with another time of year or season, but no matter when you try these Gingerbread Buckeyes, you won't be disappointed.

Gingerbread Buckeyes[12]

Ingredients

1 ¼ cups smooth unsweetened almond butter
2 tablespoons blackstrap molasses
1 tablespoon maple syrup
2 tablespoons coconut flour
1 ¼ teaspoons ground ginger
1 teaspoon cinnamon
⅛ teaspoon allspice
⅛ teaspoon nutmeg
⅛ teaspoon ground cloves
Pinch of sea salt
1 10-ounce bag dark chocolate chips
1 ½ teaspoons coconut oil

Directions

1. Combine almond butter, molasses, maple syrup, coconut flour, sea salt, and spices until fully incorporated.

2. Roll dough into roughly 1-inch balls.

3. Place rolled balls on a pan lined with parchment paper and place in the freezer for 15–20 minutes.

4. While the balls are in the freezer, melt chocolate chips in a double boiler.

5. Add coconut oil to chocolate to get desired consistency.

6. Using toothpicks, pick up the gingerbread balls and dip them into the melted chocolate. Be careful not to dip

the entire ball; leave a small uncovered area to make the buckeye.

7. Place the chocolate-covered balls back onto the parchment paper and refrigerate until chocolate is firm.

Banana Bread Buckeyes prove that you can turn any cake or bread into a chocolate-covered nugget of satisfaction. Although hemp hearts aren't a normal additive in the classic banana bread, the chopped hemp hearts help to hold the mixture together. In the Midwest, banana bread is synonymous with Bob Evans restaurants, but after making these Banana Bread Buckeyes, you'll have a new perspective on the best way to eat bananas.

Banana Bread Buckeyes[13]

Ingredients

¼ cup hemp hearts
¾ cup blanched almond flour
1 ripe banana
¼ cup natural peanut butter
3 tablespoons agave nectar
1 tablespoon coconut oil, melted and divided
½ cup walnuts, chopped
½ cup dark chocolate chips, melted
1 tablespoon flaked sea salt (garnish)
1 tablespoon hemp hearts (garnish)

Directions

1. Pulse hemp hearts and almond flour in a food processor until chopped and combined.

2. Remove from food processor and place in a separate bowl.

3. Blend banana, peanut butter, agave, and half the coconut oil in the food processor.

4. Add in walnuts and flour mixture and blend again.

5. Refrigerate for 30 minutes.

6. Roll dough into roughly 1-inch balls.

7. Place rolled balls on a pan lined with parchment paper and place in the freezer for 15–20 minutes.

8. While the balls are in the freezer, melt chocolate chips in a double boiler.

9. Add the remaining coconut oil to chocolate to get desired consistency.

10. Using toothpicks, pick up the banana bread balls and dip them into the melted chocolate. Be careful not to dip the entire ball; leave a small uncovered area to make the buckeye.

11. Place the chocolate-covered balls back onto the parchment paper.

12. Sprinkle with salt and hemp hearts.

13. Refrigerate until chocolate is firm.

I've only ever used tahini to make hummus. I know tahini has many other culinary uses, but in the Midwest, tahini is an underused recipe additive. These Tahini Buckeyes bring a little taste of the Mediterranean into your home. Raise or lower the amount of powdered sugar in the recipe based on your desired level of sweetness. You can also substitute the coconut oil with sesame oil if you want to bring in more of a nutty flavor.

Tahini Buckeyes[14]

Ingredients

¾ cup tahini
1 stick unsalted butter
3 cups powdered sugar
1 teaspoon vanilla
½ teaspoon kosher salt
2 cups dark chocolate chips
2 tablespoons coconut oil

Directions

1. Combine tahini, butter, powdered sugar, salt, and vanilla until fully incorporated.

2. Chill for 30 minutes.

3. Roll dough into roughly 1-inch balls.

4. Place rolled balls on a pan lined with parchment paper and place in the freezer for 15–20 minutes.

5. While the balls are in the freezer, melt chocolate chips in a double boiler.

6. Add coconut oil to chocolate to get desired consistency.

7. Using toothpicks, pick up the tahini balls and dip them into the melted chocolate. Be careful not to dip the entire ball; leave a small uncovered area to make the buckeye.

8. Place the chocolate-covered balls back onto the parchment paper and refrigerate until chocolate is firm.

Harvest Buckeyes allow you to experience the earthy feel of a midwestern autumn. With pumpkin puree and cannellini beans, this recipe steers far away from the chocolate and peanut-buttery origins of the original buckeye candy. But for those health-conscious or adventurous buckeye lovers among you, this may end up being your

favorite buckeye candy recipe of them all. Try this recipe during the fall or decorate your Thanksgiving table with harvest buckeyes for some added seasonal fun.

Harvest Buckeyes[15]

Ingredients

1 14-ounce can cannellini beans
½ cup unsweetened applesauce
½ cup pumpkin puree
2 tablespoons coconut oil
1 tablespoon vanilla extract
1 cup creamy peanut butter
Pinch of sea salt
1 10-ounce bag vegan chocolate chips

Directions

1. Drain and rinse the beans.

2. In a food processor, puree beans. Add applesauce, pumpkin, coconut oil, and vanilla. Puree until smooth.

3. Add peanut butter and salt and blend until fully incorporated.

4. Roll dough into roughly 1-inch balls.

5. Place rolled balls on a pan lined with parchment paper and place in the freezer for 15–20 minutes.

6. While the balls are in the freezer, melt chocolate chips in a double boiler.

7. Using toothpicks, pick up the balls and dip them into the melted chocolate. Be careful not to dip the entire ball; leave a small uncovered area to make the buckeye.

8. Place the chocolate-covered balls back onto the wax paper and refrigerate until chocolate is firm.

Who doesn't love a little toffee? The addition of chopped Heath toffee bars adds depth to this classic buckeye recipe. Your choice of toffee candy matters, and this recipe will take on the flavor characteristics of your chosen toffee. Try mixing in different toffees until you find your favorite. My personal favorite is caramel toffee. The caramel flavors are a perfect complement to the peanut butter and chocolate, but I also hear cookies-n-cream toffee taste wonderful.

Toffee Buckeyes

Ingredients

1 cup peanut butter
1 teaspoon vanilla
Pinch of kosher salt
1 cup powdered sugar
¾ cup chopped toffee candy bars
12 ounces semisweet chocolate, chopped

Directions

1. Combine peanut butter, salt, powdered sugar, and vanilla until fully incorporated.

2. Mix in the toffee pieces by hand.

3. Roll dough into roughly 1-inch balls.

4. Place rolled balls on a pan lined with parchment paper and place in the freezer for 15–20 minutes.

5. While the balls are in the freezer, melt chocolate chips in a double boiler.

6. Using toothpicks, pick up the peanut butter balls and dip them into the melted chocolate. Be careful not to dip the entire ball; leave a small uncovered area to make the buckeye.

7. Place the chocolate-covered balls back onto the parchment paper and refrigerate until chocolate is firm.

I once worked at a church where I had more than 125 volunteers on my Foreverland Children's ministry team. Each Christmas, my staff and I would make hundreds of buckeyes for the Foreverland volunteers. This is the recipe we used to make the buckeyes, and it is my personal favorite of any recipe in the book. The paraffin wax helps the chocolate to coat the peanut butter balls perfectly. It also allows the chocolate to firm up with a shiny coating. For me, buckeyes don't taste right without the wax.

Foreverland Buckeyes[16]

Ingredients

3 pounds confectioners' sugar
2 pounds creamy peanut butter
¾ cake of paraffin wax
1 pound margarine, softened
2 10-ounce packages semisweet chocolate chips

Directions

1. Blend softened margarine and peanut butter. Add ⅓ of confectioners' sugar at a time, mixing well before adding more until fully combined.

2. Refrigerate the mixture for several hours until dough is cold.

3. Remove from refrigerator and form the dough into small balls. Place balls on wax paper.

4. Once balls are formed, place them in the freezer for approximately 15 minutes.

5. While the balls are in the freezer, melt two packages of semisweet chocolate chips and ¾ cake of paraffin wax in a double boiler.

6. Using toothpicks, pick up the peanut butter balls and dip them into the melted chocolate. Be careful not to dip the entire ball; leave a small uncovered area to make the buckeye.

7. Place the chocolate-covered balls back onto the wax paper and then return to refrigerator until chocolate is firm and set.

The hardest part about making this recipe is not eating the cookie dough. If you can resist the temptation to indulge in the ingredients beforehand, you'll create some Cookie Dough Buckeyes that will delight your tummy and satisfy any party guests. This recipe seems to be a big hit with young children, especially when M&M's are used in the ingredients. If you make a double or triple batch, try mixing different mini candies in each one and taste the differences.

Cookie Dough Buckeyes[17]

Ingredients

COOKIE DOUGH
¼ cup butter, softened
2 tablespoons sugar
¼ cup brown sugar
¼ teaspoon vanilla
2 tablespoons milk
¾ cup flour
¼ cup mini candies (Reese's Pieces, M&M's, chocolate chips)

PEANUT BUTTER FILLING
1 ½ cups creamy peanut butter
½ cup butter, softened
1 teaspoon vanilla
½ teaspoon salt
3 cups powdered sugar

FOR COATING
12 ounces semisweet chocolate chips
3–4 ounces (or ¼ of a standard block) paraffin wax

Directions

1. Combine all cookie dough ingredients in a bowl. Mix thoroughly until well combined.

2. Roll cookie dough into roughly 1-inch balls.

3. Place rolled balls on a pan lined with parchment paper and place in the freezer for 15–20 minutes.

4. While cookie dough chills, combine peanut butter, butter, powdered sugar, vanilla, and salt until fully incorporated.

5. Make balls out of 2 tablespoons of the mixture and flatten.

6. Place a frozen cookie doughball in the center of the flattened peanut butter mixture and then use the peanut butter mixture to wrap around the frozen cookie dough ball. Once all balls are made, place in freezer for 15 minutes.

7. While the balls are in the freezer, melt chocolate chips in a double boiler. Add ½ inch of wax to smooth and firm up the finished chocolate.

8. Using toothpicks, pick up the peanut butter balls and dip them into the melted chocolate. Be careful not to dip the entire ball; leave a small uncovered area to make the buckeye.

9. Place the chocolate-covered balls back onto the parchment paper and refrigerate until chocolate is firm.

This recipe is for all the chocolate chip cookie fans. It replaces the standard peanut butter ingredient with chocolate chip cookie dough. If you have ever thought that you'd love to have a chocolate chip cookie coated in chocolate, then this recipe is sure to be a winner. The best part about this recipe is you don't have to heat up the oven or wait for your cookies to cool on the racks. You can experience all the satisfaction of a chocolate chip cookie without the baking.

Chocolate Chip Cookie Dough Buckeyes[18]

Ingredients

½ cup butter, softened
¾ cup brown sugar
¼ cup milk
1 teaspoon vanilla
½ teaspoon salt
1 ¼ cups all-purpose flour
1 cup mini chocolate chips
16 ounces candy chocolate

Directions

1. Combine brown sugar and butter until smooth. Add milk, vanilla, salt, flour, and chocolate chips until fully incorporated.

2. Roll dough into roughly 1-inch balls.

3. Place rolled balls on a pan lined with parchment paper and place in the freezer for 15–20 minutes.

4. While the balls are in the freezer, melt candy chocolate according to package directions.

5. Using toothpicks, pick up the cookie doughballs and dip them into the melted chocolate. Be careful not to dip the entire ball; leave a small uncovered area to make the buckeye.

6. Place the chocolate-covered balls back onto the parchment paper and refrigerate until chocolate is firm.

Crunchy peanut butter alone doesn't always provide the most crunch. By adding in crisped rice cereal, you can increase the amount of crunch in your buckeye candies. Fans of Nestlé Crunch bars will love this version of buckeyes. You can choose between adding crunchy or smooth

peanut butter to increase or decrease the amount of texture in your Crunchy Buckeyes. These buckeyes make the perfect snack when you want a buckeye, but don't want it as sweet as the standard recipe.

Crunchy Buckeyes[19]

Ingredients

¼ cup butter, softened
1 ¼ cups peanut butter (crunchy or smooth)
1 teaspoon vanilla
1 cup powdered sugar
1 ½ cups crisped rice cereal
2 cups semisweet chocolate (chopped)
1–2 tablespoons coconut oil

Directions

1. Combine peanut butter, butter, powdered sugar, and vanilla in a bowl until fully incorporated.

2. Add the crisped rice cereal until well mixed.

3. Roll dough into roughly 1-inch balls.

4. Place rolled balls on a pan lined with parchment paper and place in the freezer for 15–20 minutes.

5. While the balls are in the freezer, melt chocolate chips in a double boiler.

6. Add coconut oil to chocolate to get desired consistency.

7. Using toothpicks, pick up the peanut butter balls and dip them into the melted chocolate. Be careful not to dip the entire ball; leave a small uncovered area to make the buckeye.

8. Place the chocolate-covered balls back onto the parchment paper and refrigerate until chocolate is firm.

Buckeye Cakes and Dessert Recipes

In the dessert world, the term *buckeye* has become synonymous with saying "chocolate and peanut butter." Any dessert concocted with a combination of these two ingredients is a buckeye. Peanut butter and chocolate are a match made in heaven, and the recipes beyond allow you to experience the buckeye flavors in many different shapes and sizes. Enjoy the brownies, cakes, cookies, and more and use these recipes to make a startling buckeye dish for your next party or potluck.

The only thing that can make chocolate-covered pretzels any better—adding peanut butter. Buckeye Pretzels are a flavor explosion in your mouth, from the juxtaposition of salt and sweet to the texture differences of hard pretzels and creamy peanut butter. These treats make great everyday snacks. They also are the perfect accompaniments for a long road trip. Take a container—you won't regret it.

Buckeye Pretzels[20]

Ingredients

1 cup peanut butter
2 tablespoons butter, softened
Dash of salt
½ teaspoon vanilla
1 ¼ cups powdered sugar
Pretzels, waffle shaped
12 ounces chocolate (CandiQuik)

Directions

1. Combine peanut butter, butter, salt, and vanilla in a bowl until fully incorporated.

2. Add the powdered sugar until well mixed.

3. Roll dough into roughly 1-inch balls.

4. Place the doughball between two waffle-shaped pretzels and press together to make a block shape.

5. Place pretzel blocks on a pan lined with parchment paper and place in the freezer for 15–20 minutes.

6. While the blocks are in the freezer, melt chocolate chips according to the package directions.

7. Dip the pretzel blocks halfway into the melted chocolate. Be careful not to dip the entire block; leave a small uncovered area to make the buckeye.

8. Place the chocolate-covered blocks back onto the parchment paper and refrigerate until chocolate is firm.

These Buckeye Crunch Bars are the hit of every potluck. This recipe is reminiscent of a Nestlé Crunch bar dipped in peanut butter—but you can make it by the pan. I prefer the creamy peanut butter instead of the crunchy peanut butter in this recipe. The creamy peanut butter allows all the crunchy goodness to be focused on the addition of the Nestlé Buncha Crunch.

Buckeye Crunch Bars[21]

Ingredients

¾ cup unsalted butter, melted
3 ½ cups powdered sugar
1 ½ cups peanut butter, creamy or crunchy
1 teaspoon vanilla
2 9-ounce pouches Nestlé Buncha Crunch (or 1 cup chopped Crunch bars)
1 ½ tablespoons unsalted butter

Directions

1. Line a square 13-by-9-inch pan with foil.

2. Combine peanut butter, ¾ cup melted butter, powdered sugar, and vanilla in a bowl until fully incorporated.

3. Press the dough firmly into the foil-lined pan.

4. Place dough in the freezer for 15–20 minutes.

5. While the dough is in the freezer, microwave chocolate and remaining butter in 30-second intervals, stirring until the chocolate mixture is easy to stir.

6. Remove buckeye dough from freezer and coat with the chocolate.

7. Chill for an hour before serving.

Yes, you can have buckeyes if you are gluten-free. These Gluten-Free Buckeye Brownies will melt your taste buds and keep you from being jealous of any of the gluten options. Just because something is gluten-free doesn't mean it has to taste bad. You can play around with different gluten-free flours until you find your favorite. In my experience, almond flour or banana flour makes a perfect gluten-free substitute.

Gluten-Free Buckeye Brownies[22]

Ingredients

BROWNIES

⅓ cup dutch cocoa

½ cup plus 2 tablespoons boiling water

2 ounces unsweetened chocolate, finely chopped

4 tablespoons unsalted butter, melted

½ cup plus 2 tablespoons canola oil

2 large eggs

2 large egg yolks

2 teaspoons vanilla

2 ½ cups sugar

1 ¾ cups all-purpose gluten-free flour

½ teaspoon xanthan gum (only if your flour doesn't already have xanthan or guar gum)

¾ teaspoon salt

PEANUT BUTTER LAYER

¾ cup creamy peanut butter

½ cup unsalted butter

⅛ teaspoon salt

2 ¼ cups powdered sugar

2 tablespoons whole milk

1 teaspoon vanilla

CHOCOLATE PEANUT BUTTER GLAZE

1 ½ cups semisweet chocolate chips

⅓ cup creamy peanut butter

Directions

Preheat oven to 350 degrees Fahrenheit and grease a
13-by-9-inch pan.

1. Combine cocoa and boiling water until smooth. Add in
   unsweetened chocolate and mix until melted.

2. Mix in melted butter and oil. Once mixed, add eggs,
   yolks, and vanilla, and continue mix until smooth.

3. Add sugar and mix until fully incorporated.

4. In a separate bowl, combine gluten-free flour, xanthan
   gum, and salt.

5. Mix flour mixture with the cocoa mixture until well
   mixed.

6. Place mixture in prepared pan and cook for 30–35
   minutes until an inserted toothpick comes out clean.

7. While pan cools, combine peanut butter, butter, and
   salt in a stand mixer until smooth.

8. Add in powdered sugar, vanilla, and milk until fully
   incorporated.

9. Spread mixture evenly over the brownies. Set aside.

10. Microwave the chocolate chips and peanut butter in
    30-second intervals, stirring until smooth.

11. Pour chocolate mixture on top of brownies.

12. Chill for 30 minutes before serving.

I gave you the recipe for Healthy Buckeye Balls, so I have to give you a recipe for Healthy Buckeye Bars too, right? This recipe doesn't sacrifice flavor for the sake of just being healthy. If you serve this at an event or gathering, most of your guests won't even know that it is a healthier option—but you will, and your waistline will too.

Healthy Buckeye Bars[23]

Ingredients

PEANUT BUTTER LAYER
1 ¼ cups natural peanut butter (creamy or crunchy)
⅓ cup coconut oil, softened
¼ cup real maple syrup or light agave nectar

CHOCOLATE LAYER
⅓ cup coconut oil, melted
⅓ cup cocoa powder
¼ cup real maple syrup or light agave nectar
½ teaspoon vanilla

Directions

1. Line a square 13-by-9-inch pan with wax paper.

2. Combine peanut butter, coconut oil, and maple syrup or agave nectar in a bowl until fully incorporated.

3. Press the dough firmly into the wax paper–lined pan.

4. Place dough in the freezer for 15–20 minutes.

5. While the dough is in the freezer, mix cocoa powder, coconut oil, vanilla, and maple syrup or agave nectar in a small bowl until well mixed.

6. Remove buckeye dough from freezer and coat with the chocolate.

7. Chill for an hour before serving.

Bundt cake may not be your go-to dessert for family gatherings or functions, but with this recipe, you may rethink that. Buckeye Bundt Cake mixes a chocolate cake with a peanut butter, cream cheese, and powdered sugar filling. If that doesn't sound good enough, it is all topped off with a chocolate glaze. This Bundt cake may take a few steps to create, but this dessert is sure to become a family favorite.

Buckeye Bundt Cake[24]

Ingredients

FILLING

¾ cup creamy peanut butter

4 ounces cream cheese, room temperature

¼ cup powdered sugar

1 egg

3 tablespoons milk

CAKE

1 ¾ cups all-purpose flour

½ teaspoon baking soda

½ teaspoon salt

¾ cup cocoa powder

¾ cup water, boiling

3 ounces semisweet chocolate, chopped

¾ cup plain greek yogurt

12 tablespoons unsalted butter, softened

1 ⅔ cups brown sugar

2 eggs

2 teaspoons vanilla

½ cup heavy cream

1 tablespoon sugar

2 tablespoons corn syrup

¼ cup creamy peanut butter

4 ounces semisweet chocolate, finely chopped

Directions

1. Preheat oven to 350 degrees Fahrenheit.

2. Grease a 10- to 12-cup Bundt pan. Coat pan evenly with cocoa powder.

3. In a bowl, combine peanut butter, cream cheese, powdered sugar, egg, and milk until smooth.

4. Place filling into a pastry bag and set aside in refrigerator.

5. In a separate bowl, combine, flour, baking, soda, and salt. Set aside.

6. In another bowl, mix boiling water with cocoa powder. Add in chocolate and stir until smooth.

7. Mix in greek yogurt and combine until well integrated. Set the cocoa-yogurt mix aside.

8. In large mixing bowl, combine butter and sugar. Add eggs and vanilla. Alternating ingredients, mix in the cocoa-yogurt mixture and the flour mixture until fully incorporated.

9. Pour ¾ of the batter into prepared pan.

10. Squeeze the peanut butter filing into a ring in the center of the chocolate batter.

11. Pour the remaining batter on top.

12. Bake 50–60 minutes until an inserted toothpick comes out clean.

13. Remove from oven and cool for 10 minutes before removing from pan.

14. To make the glaze, heat cream, sugar, and corn syrup on the stove on medium-high heat. Once simmering, remove from heat and add in chocolate and stir until melted. Add peanut butter and stir until smooth.

15. Pour mixture over Bundt cake and let cool before serving.

Rice Krispies bars are one of easiest desserts you can make. The simple combination of marshmallow and Rice Krispies cereal creates a crunchy treat that sticks to your fingers and roof of your mouth. How do you improve a classic dessert like that? You add a layer of peanut butter dough on top and then coat it with chocolate. Make sure you purchase the name-brand cereal. The generic brands often turn soggy and stale faster.

Buckeyes Rice Krispies[25]

Ingredients

PEANUT BUTTER RICE KRISPIES
10 ounces mini marshmallows
4 tablespoons butter
½ teaspoon vanilla
½ cup peanut butter (Reese's)
6–7 cups Rice Krispies cereal

PEANUT BUTTER LAYER
2 cups powdered sugar
1 cup peanut butter (Reese's)
½ cup butter, softened

CHOCOLATE PEANUT BUTTER LAYER

1 cup 60 percent semisweet chocolate chips (Ghirardelli)

1 cup peanut butter chocolate chips (Reese's)

¼ cup peanut butter (Reese's)

Directions

1. Grease a 13-by-9-inch pan and set aside.

2. Melt butter on the stove in a large pan. Once melted, add in the marshmallows. Stir until melted.

3. Add in the peanut butter and vanilla until fully incorporated.

4. Stir in Rice Krispies until well mixed.

5. Place mixture in the greased pan and let cool for 15 minutes.

6. While the Rice Krispies mixture is cooling, combine peanut butter, ½ cup butter, and powdered sugar in a bowl until smooth.

7. Press the dough firmly into the pan on top of the Rice Krispies mixture.

8. Place pan in the freezer until the chocolate is ready.

9. While the dough is in the freezer, microwave chocolate and peanut butter chips in 30-second intervals, stirring until the chocolate mixture is easy to stir.

10. Add peanut butter and stir until smooth.

11. Evenly spread chocolate layer on top on the chilled pan of peanut butter dough.

12. Chill for 30 minutes before serving.

Caramel makes everything taste better. Buckeye Turtle Brownies combine the gooey sweetness of caramel with the salty crunch of pecans. Add in the peanut butter and chocolate, and your mouth will

experience a smorgasbord of flavors. This recipe is quick to make.
Make sure to buy a high-quality box of brownie mix. I prefer brownie
mixes with chocolate syrup additives, but if you can't find any of those,
you can always add a couple handfuls of chocolate chips to the batter.
Follow the directions on the box to make a fudgy brownie and not a
cakey one. Cakey brownies are too dry for this recipe.

Buckeye Turtle Brownies[26]

Ingredients

BROWNIES
1 box of brownie mix

TURTLE TOPPING
11-ounce bag of caramels, unwrapped
2 tablespoons milk
1 ½ cups pecans, chopped

PEANUT BUTTER TOPPING
6 tablespoons butter, softened
¾ cup creamy peanut butter
1 ½ cups powdered sugar
1 ½ tablespoons milk

CHOCOLATE TOPPING
1 cup semisweet chocolate chips
1 ½ teaspoons vegetable oil
Sea salt, coarse

Directions

1. Prepare brownies according to the directions on the box.

2. Let brownies cool completely.

3. Microwave caramels and milk in 30-second intervals, stirring until smooth.

4. Remove bowl from microwave and add in pecans.

5. Spread caramel mixture evenly over cooled brownies.

6. In a separate bowl, combine butter, peanut butter, powdered sugar, and milk until well mixed.

7. Spread peanut butter mixture evenly over caramel layer.

8. In a separate bowl, microwave chocolate chips and vegetable oil in 30-sceond increments, stirring until smooth.

9. Pour chocolate layer on top of peanut butter layer.

10. Sprinkle with sea salt and chill until chocolate in set.

When you need a quick buckeye fix, this is the recipe for you. If you don't want to crush up your own Oreos, you can buy a premade Oreo pie crust. This is a great dessert for when you don't know what to make for a party and don't really want to spend much time thinking through one. If you keep Oreo pie crusts in your cupboard, this can be your default buckeye dish.

Buckeye Pie[27]

Ingredients

20 Oreos, crushed
3 tablespoons butter, melted
½ cup butter, softened
1 ⅔ cups creamy peanut butter
1 ¼ cups powdered sugar
1 teaspoon kosher salt
½ teaspoon vanilla
1 ½ cups chocolate chips
¾ cup heavy cream

Directions

1. Combine crushed Oreos and melted butter in a large bowl.

2. Firmly press mixture into a pie dish.

3. With a hand mixer, combine peanut butter, butter, powdered sugar, vanilla, and salt in a bowl until whipped.

4. Spread whipped mixture evenly on top of the Oreo crust.

5. Place in the freezer for 15–20 minutes.

6. While the pie chills, heat cream on the stove until it begins to simmer. Remove from heat and pour over chocolate chips in a heat-safe bowl. Let stand for 5 minutes before stirring until smooth.

7. Pour chocolate over the peanut butter pie.

8. Chill for an hour before serving.

Buckeye Brownie Cheesecake is an advanced dessert recipe not for the faint of heart. Don't try this recipe first unless you are an established baker. The taste of this cheesecake is out of this world, but it comes with a lengthy creation process. If you invest the time and energy to create this cheesecake, you and your family and friends will be duly rewarded. If you are a novice baker, maybe start with the Mini Buckeye Cheesecake first.

Buckeye Brownie Cheesecake[28]

Ingredients

BROWNIE CRUST
4 ounces bittersweet chocolate
½ cup unsalted butter
¼ teaspoon salt
⅔ cup sugar
1 teaspoon vanilla
2 eggs
¾ cup flour
8 buckeye candies, pieces

PEANUT BUTTER CHEESECAKE

16 ounces cream cheese, softened

½ cup sugar

¾ cup peanut butter

2 teaspoons cornstarch

¾ cup heavy cream

Pinch of salt

1 teaspoon vanilla

3 eggs

CHOCOLATE GANACHE

12 ounces semisweet chocolate

1 cup heavy cream

Pinch of salt

PEANUT BUTTER TOPPING

¼ cup butter

Pinch of salt

¾ cup peanut butter

¾ cup powdered sugar

Buckeye candies (garnish)

Directions

BROWNIE BOTTOM

1. Preheat the oven to 350 degrees Fahrenheit.

2. Butter a 9-inch springform pan.

3. Microwave chocolate, butter, and salt together in 30-second increments. Stir until smooth.

4. Add in sugar and vanilla and stir until smooth. Mix in the eggs, one at a time, until well mixed.

5. Stir in flour until thoroughly mixed and fold in the buckeye candy pieces. Pour mixture in the springform pan and bake for 15 minutes.

6. Remove from oven and let cool.

PEANUT BUTTER CHEESECAKE

1. Set oven temperature to 300 degrees Fahrenheit.

2. Combine cream cheese and sugar until smooth.

3. Add in peanut butter, cream, cornstarch, salt, and vanilla until well mixed.

4. Add in eggs, one at a time, until fully incorporated.

5. Pour cheesecake mixture over the brownie bottom.

6. Wrap the springform pan in aluminum foil. Place pan in a larger pan filled with hot water. Do not allow water to seep into the springform pan.

7. Bake for 60–70 minutes.

8. Turn off the oven and let the cheesecake cool in the oven for 30 minutes with the oven door slightly ajar.

9. Separate pans and let cheesecake cool for 3–4 hours.

10. Once cooled, remove from springform pan.

TOPPING

1. Melt peanut butter and butter together in 30-second intervals, stirring until smooth.

2. Add salt and powdered sugar and mix until smooth.

3. Spread over the top of the cheesecake.

4. In a separate bowl, microwave cream, chocolate, and salt in 30-second intervals, stirring until smooth.

5. Once cool, spread around the outside of the cheesecake.

6. Add buckeye candies for garnish.

This Mini Buckeye Cheesecake recipe is the best recipe for novice bakers to experience the delicacy of buckeyes mixed with cheesecake. All you need is a muffin pan and some liners, and you can create the perfect buckeye cheesecakes. The peanut garnish is optional. I suggest

leaving it off until you determine if you like the added crunch. Some people won't like the stark contrast of hard peanuts mixed with the soft cheesecake. It's best to figure out first what your audience likes before adding the nuts.

Mini Buckeye Cheesecake[29]

Ingredients

1 cup chocolate graham crackers, finely crushed

3 tablespoons unsalted butter, melted

16 ounces cream cheese, softened

½ cup peanut butter

⅔ cup granulated sugar

1 tablespoon flour

1 teaspoon vanilla

2 eggs

12 ounces semisweet chocolate chips

½ cup heavy cream

¼ cup peanuts, finely crushed (garnish)

Directions

1. Preheat the oven to 350 degrees Fahrenheit.

2. Line muffin pan with 12 cupcake liners.

3. Mix graham cracker crumbs and butter in a bowl. Fill bottom third of cupcake liners with graham cracker crust. Press firm to the bottom.

4. In a separate bowl or mixer, combine cream cheese, peanut butter, sugar, flour, and vanilla until well mixed.

5. Add in eggs, one at a time, until fully incorporated.

6. Pour on top of crust and fill cupcake liners ⅔ full.

7. Bake for 18–22 minutes.

8. While cheesecakes are cooling, in a separate bowl, microwave cream and chocolate in 30-second intervals, stirring until smooth.

9. Pour a layer of chocolate on top of cheesecakes and add peanuts for garnish.

No-Bake Buckeyes remind me of my Ohio high school. We had similar desserts in our cafeteria, and I would eat them almost every day. With only four ingredients, this is one of the simplest recipes in this book. You can make it with children, and if you keep the four ingredients well stocked in your pantry, No-Bake Buckeyes can quickly become a staple in your buckeye dessert repertoire.

No-Bake Buckeyes[30]

Ingredients

2 cups low-sugar vanilla frosting
1 ½ cups creamy peanut butter
1 ½ cups chocolate chips
1 tablespoon butter

Directions

1. Line a 13-by-9-inch pan with parchment paper.

2. Microwave peanut butter and frosting in 30-second intervals, mixing until fully incorporated.

3. Pour melted peanut butter into the pan.

4. Place pan in the freezer for 15–20 minutes.

5. While the pan is in the freezer, melt chocolate and butter in 30-second intervals, stirring until well mixed.

6. Remove pan from freezer and coat with the chocolate.

7. Chill for an hour before serving.

This allergy-free version of the No-Bake Buckeyes still only includes four ingredients, but it allows people with peanut or dairy allergies to enjoy the midwestern delicacy. If you don't have a dairy allergy,

you can substitute real butter for this recipe. The same can be said if you don't have a peanut allergy—you can swap the ingredient out. The most important thing to remember for Allergy-Free No-Bake Buckeyes is to read the ingredient list on the chocolate. Make sure to purchase a nut-free and dairy-free chocolate.

Allergy-Free No-Bake Buckeyes[31]

Ingredients

2 cups low-sugar vanilla frosting
1 ½ cups sunflower butter
1 ½ cups chocolate chips
1 tablespoon dairy-free butter

Directions

1. Line a 13-by-9-inch pan with parchment paper.

2. Microwave sunflower butter and frosting in 30-second intervals, mixing until fully incorporated.

3. Pour melted sunflower butter into the pan.

4. Place pan in the freezer for 15–20 minutes.

5. While the pan is in the freezer, melt chocolate and butter in 30-second intervals, stirring until well mixed.

6. Remove pan from freezer and coat with the chocolate.

7. Chill for an hour before serving.

Brownies have always been one of my favorite desserts. Transforming brownies into a variety of other desserts never gets old. This recipe for Buckeye Brownies provides all the information to make your own "from scratch" brownies. You can also pick up your favorite brownie mix from the local grocery store if you don't have time to make the brownie layer from scratch. As with other brownie recipes, make sure to slightly undercook the brownies to give them a fudgy texture.

Buckeye Brownies[32]

Ingredients

BROWNIE LAYER

1 cup butter

1 ¼ cups sugar

1 cup lightly packed dark brown sugar

1 tablespoon espresso powder

1 teaspoon vanilla

1 cup dark chocolate cocoa powder

4 large eggs

1 ¼ cups flour

1 teaspoon baking powder

½ teaspoon salt

10-ounce bag Hershey's Mini Kisses

PEANUT BUTTER LAYER

½ cup unsalted butter, softened

½ cup creamy peanut butter

2 cups powdered sugar

1 teaspoon vanilla

2 tablespoons heavy cream

Pinch of salt

CHOCOLATE LAYER

300g Lindt 50 percent chocolate (3 100g bars), chopped

⅓ cup creamy peanut butter, heaping

Directions

1. Preheat oven to 350 degrees Fahrenheit.

2. Line 13-by-9-inch pan with parchment paper.

3. On the stove, melt butter over medium-high heat. Stir in cocoa powder, espresso powder, and vanilla until smooth. Remove from stove to cool.

4. In a bowl, combine brown sugar and sugar. Add in cooled chocolate mixture and stir until well combined.

5. Add eggs, one at a time, until fully incorporated.

6. In a separate bowl, mix flour, salt, and baking powder together.

7. Stir flour mixture into the chocolate mixture.

8. Fold in Mini Kisses.

9. Pour evenly into the 13-by-9-inch pan.

10. Bake for 27–30 minutes until an inserted toothpick comes out clean.

11. Leave in pan until cooled.

PEANUT BUTTER LAYER

1. In a stand mixer, mix butter and peanut butter until smooth.

2. Add powdered sugar, vanilla, and salt and mix until smooth.

3. Add heavy cream and mix on high for 2 minutes.

4. Evenly spread peanut butter filling over cooled brownie.

CHOCOLATE LAYER

1. On the stove, melt chopped chocolate and peanut butter over medium-low heat. Stir until chocolate is melted and smooth.

2. Remove from stove and allow to cool.

3. Pour cooled chocolate evenly on top of the peanut butter layer.

4. Chill before serving.

Brownie cookies? Yes, you can take brownie mix and turn it into cookies. And when you add peanut butter and chocolate, you can turn those little cookies into a buckeye dessert that will make every mouth happy. For this recipe, don't buy brownie mix that includes additional chocolate, such as chocolate syrup or chips. You can purchase a generic box of brownies for Buckeye Brownie Cookies; the brand doesn't matter for how you are going to use the brownie mix in this recipe.

Buckeye Brownie Cookies[33]

Ingredients

1 box (18–19 ounces) brownie mix
¼ cup butter, melted
½ cup cream cheese, softened
1 egg
¾ cup peanut butter
¾ cup powdered sugar
¾ cup chocolate frosting
Topping
1 cup milk chocolate chips
¼ cup butter

Directions

1. Preheat oven to 350 degrees Fahrenheit.

2. Line a baking sheet with parchment paper.

3. Combine brownie mix, butter, cream cheese, and egg until well mixed.

4. Roll dough into 1-inch balls and place on baking sheet, 2 inches apart. Push your thumb into the center to make an indent.

5. In another bowl, combine peanut butter and powdered sugar. Roll dough into ½-inch balls and place in the indent of each cookie.

6. Bake for 10–12 minutes.

7. While cookies cool, melt chocolate chips and butter in 30-second intervals, stirring until well mixed.

8. Coat cooled cookies with chocolate frosting and then drizzle with melted chocolate.

These Buckeye Thumbprint Cookies are as easy to make as their name suggests. After mixing all the ingredients together in a bowl, you roll the mixture into little balls and place them on a cookie sheet. Before you put the doughballs in the oven, you press your finger into each one to leave a fingerprint-shaped indent. Typically, thumbprint cookies stop there, but with the buckeye variation, you get to load that thumb indent with peanut butter filling and then drizzle it with chocolate. What's not to love about these thumbprint cookies?

Buckeye Thumbprint Cookies[34]

Ingredients

1 cup butter, softened
1 cup sugar
1 large egg yolk
1 teaspoon vanilla
2 cups all-purpose flour
½ cup unsweetened cocoa powder
½ teaspoon salt

PEANUT BUTTER FILLING
½ cup creamy peanut butter
½ cup powdered sugar
1 teaspoon vanilla
4 ounces semisweet baking chocolate, chopped (garnish)

Directions

1. Preheat oven to 350 degrees Fahrenheit.

2. Line a baking sheet with parchment paper.

3. Combine peanut butter, butter, and powdered sugar until smooth. Set aside.

4. Using another bowl, mix butter and sugar until smooth. Add in egg yolk and vanilla until well mixed.

5. In a separate bowl, combine flour, cocoa powder, and salt. Add this mixture to the butter and sugar bowl to make the dough.

6. Roll dough into 1-inch balls and place on baking sheet 2 inches apart. Push your thumb into the center to make an indent.

7. Fill the indent with a spoonful of the peanut butter filling.

8. Bake for 15 minutes.

9. While cookies cool, melt baking chocolate chips in 30-second intervals, stirring until smooth.

10. Drizzle cooled cookies with melted chocolate.

Ever had a stuffed cookie cake? No? Most people haven't either, so don't worry about it. With the Buckeye Stuffed Cookie Cake, you can create a unique dessert that your dinner guests and family will be talking about for months. This recipe calls for the use of springform pans. You can try to make it without the springform pans, but I don't recommend it. The pans just make everything easier, and since this recipe has lots of steps, I don't suggest making it any more difficult.

Buckeye Stuffed Cookie Cake[35]

Ingredients

COOKIE CAKE
1 ¼ cups all-purpose flour
½ cup cocoa powder
1 teaspoon baking soda
1 teaspoon salt

½ cup (1 stick) unsalted butter, melted

1 cup light brown sugar, lightly packed

¾ cup creamy peanut butter

1 egg

½ tablespoon vanilla

1 cup semisweet chocolate chips

FILLING

¾ cup creamy peanut butter

½ cup (1 stick) unsalted butter, softened

½ teaspoon vanilla

3 cups powdered sugar

FROSTING

½ cup powdered sugar

½ cup creamy peanut butter

2 tablespoons unsalted butter, softened

½ teaspoon vanilla

Pinch of salt

2 tablespoons heavy cream

Buckeye candies (garnish)

Directions

1. Preheat the oven to 350 degrees Fahrenheit.

2. Butter a 10-inch springform pan.

3. Combine, flour, cocoa, baking soda, and salt. Set aside.

4. In a separate bowl, combine melted butter and sugar until smooth.

5. Mix in egg, vanilla, peanut butter, flour, and baking soda mixture until fully incorporated. Fold in chocolate chips to make the cookie dough. Chill in freezer for 30 minutes.

6. While mixture is cooling, combine peanut butter, butter, vanilla, and powdered sugar until fully incorporated into a dough.

7. Roll peanut butter dough into a 10-inch disc and chill in the freezer for 30 minutes.

8. Remove cookie dough from freezer and roll into two 10-inch discs. Place one disc on the bottom of the springform pan.

9. Remove peanut butter disc from freezer and place on top of the cookie dough disc.

10. Place the remaining cookie dough disc on top.

11. Bake 18–20 minutes.

12. Let cool completely.

13. While cooling, combine powdered sugar, peanut butter, butter, vanilla, and salt in a stand mixer. Add cream and mix on high speed until smooth.

14. Frost cooled cake and garnish with buckeye candies.

This recipe is like the Taj Mahal of buckeye cakes and desserts. For this recipe you are going to make chocolate bourbon ganache and use a fancy ingredient—meringue powder. Sounds a little difficult, doesn't it? This recipe may not be for the faint of heart, but it is one of the most photographable of the buckeye recipes in the book. This cake is the perfect complement to any buckeye lover's birthday party or the perfect way to spend a cloudy midwestern day.

Buckeye Bourbon Cake[36]

Ingredients

7 ½ ounces bittersweet chocolate, chopped
1 cup unsalted butter
½ cup bourbon

1 cup strong coffee, hot

1 ½ cups sugar

4 eggs plus 2 egg yolks

¼ cup canola oil

⅔ cup plain greek yogurt

3 cups all-purpose flour

1 tablespoon baking powder

¾ cup unsweetened cocoa powder

1 teaspoon kosher salt

PEANUT BUTTER FROSTING

¼ cup peanut butter

1 cup butter, softened

1 tablespoon vanilla

2 ¼ cups powdered sugar

CHOCOLATE FROSTING

1 cup butter, softened

1 ½ cups powdered sugar

½ cup unsweetened cocoa powder

2 tablespoons meringue powder (optional)

1 tablespoon vanilla

2–4 tablespoons milk

CHOCOLATE BOURBON GANACHE

3 ounces bittersweet chocolate, chopped

4 ounces heavy cream

1 tablespoon bourbon

Buckeye candies (garnish)

Directions

1. Preheat oven to 350 degrees Fahrenheit.

2. Grease three 8-inch round cake pans.

3. For cake, combine the flour, cocoa powder, baking powder, and salt until thoroughly combined.

4. Microwave butter and chocolate in 30-second intervals, stirring until well mixed.

5. Stir in bourbon and coffee.

6. In a stand mixer, mix eggs, egg yolks, and sugar. Beat on medium-high speed until mixture is light and fluffy.

7. Add in canola oil and greek yogurt and mix until fully incorporated.

8. Slowly mix in the cooled chocolate mixture until well mixed.

9. Incorporate the flour mixture gradually until mixture is smooth.

10. Pour the cake batter equally into the three greased pans.

11. Bake each 20–25 minutes until toothpick comes out clean. Let cool for 5 minutes before removing from the pans. Place cakes in refrigerator for 1–2 hours before icing.

12. While cakes cool, combine butter and peanut butter in a stand mixer until light and fluffy.

13. Add in vanilla and powdered sugar until smooth.

14. Remove from bowl and save for later.

15. In a stand mixer, combine cocoa powder, powdered sugar, meringue powder, vanilla, and 2 tablespoons milk. Mix until light and fluffy. You can add more milk for desired thickness.

16. Retrieve the cooled cakes.

17. Coat each of the cakes in the peanut butter frosting. Stacking each cake on top of another until all three cakes are iced and stacked.

18. Spread the chocolate icing on the sides and top of stacked cake. Be careful to leave a circle of peanut

butter icing exposed on the top to resemble the buckeye nut.

19. To make the ganache, microwave the chocolate and heavy cream in 30-second intervals, stirring until well mixed. Add in the bourbon and stir until smooth.

20. Pour the melted ganache on top of the cake, leaving the buckeye spot exposed. Spread to the edges and let drip down the sides of the cake.

21. Let cake set for 30 minutes before finishing with buckeye candies.

Buckeye Drinks and Shakes Recipes

Ever wish you could drink a buckeye? I imagine not many have said yes to that question, but just in case you are curious, we have a few buckeye drink and shake recipes for you. Whether you like your drinks with a little splash of alcohol or packed to the brim with ice cream, there's something for everyone. You'll be the life of your next cocktail party or Ohio State University tailgate if you add one or more of these recipes to the menu.

Want to spice up your next cocktail party? Offer your guests a Buckeye Martini and watch them revel in the midwestern candy's unique twist on a classic mixed drink. It's important to ensure the glass and buckeye are chilled enough that your buckeye candy doesn't melt in the glass.

Buckeye Martini[37]

Ingredients

chocolate syrup (for garnish)
1 ½ ounces chocolate vodka
1 ounce peanut-flavored rum
¾ ounce chocolate liqueur

½ ounce cream

1 shaker of ice or ¼ cup ice in a blender

1 buckeye candy (for garnish)

Directions

1. On the inside of a chilled martini glass, drizzle the chocolate syrup. Place martini glass in the refrigerator until ready to use.

2. Set aside the garnish ingredients. Place all other ingredients in a shaker filled with ice.

3. Vigorously shake the shaker until all ingredients are well mixed.

4. Strain the shaker ingredients into the prepared martini glass.

5. Place the buckeye candy in the glass for garnish.

TIPS

For the richest flavor, try using Castries Peanut Rum Crème and Van Gogh Dutch Chocolate Vodka. Or you can mix it up with Roman Candy Rum's Chocolate Flavored Rum and Old School Peanut Butter Flavored Vodka.

This twist on a Buckeye Martini begins with your own version of a Homemade Reese's Vodka. You can also serve the Reese's Vodka by itself, and if you want to make it a Buckeye Vodka, just drizzle a little chocolate syrup in the martini glass before serving.

Buckeye Martini[38]
(Reese's Variation)

Ingredients

Chocolate syrup (for garnish)

1 ½ ounces homemade Reese's Vodka (recipe below)

1 ounce peanut-flavored rum

¾ ounce chocolate liqueur

½ ounce cream

1 shaker of ice or ¼ cup ice in a blender

2 small buckeye candies (for garnish)

1 skewer (for garnish)

Directions

1. On the inside of a chilled martini glass, drizzle the chocolate syrup. Place martini glass in the refrigerator until ready to use.

2. Set aside the garnish ingredients. Place all other ingredients in a shaker filled with ice.

3. Vigorously shake the shaker until all ingredients are well mixed.

4. Strain the shaker ingredients into the prepared martini glass.

5. Skewer the buckeye candies and place in the glass for garnish.

Homemade Reese's Vodka

Ingredients

2 Reese's Peanut Butter Cups

½ cup vodka

Directions

1. Blend the Reese's Peanut Butter Cups and vodka together in a blender. Blend until smooth.

2. Strain into a container and store at room temperature until ready to use.

Many people want an alcohol-free version of the Buckeye Martini. This Skinny Buckeye Mocktini not only contains no alcohol but is

also made with sugar-free syrups. If you want the full-sugar version, you can exchange the sugar-free syrups out for whichever you prefer. You can serve this mocktini at family functions to both children and adults—it is safe for every age group.

Skinny Buckeye Mocktini[39]

Ingredients

1 tablespoon sugar-free chocolate syrup (Torani; garnish)
½ cup almond milk
2 tablespoons heavy cream
1 tablespoon unsweetened cocoa powder
3 tablespoons sugar-free peanut butter syrup (Torani)
1 tablespoon powdered peanut butter
2 sugar-free buckeye candies (garnish)
1 ½ ounces vodka (optional)

Directions

1. On the inside of a chilled martini glass, drizzle the sugar-free chocolate syrup. Place martini glass in the refrigerator until ready to use.

2. Set aside the garnish ingredients. Place all other ingredients in a shaker filled with ice. If you want to make a Skinny Buckeye Martini, add the optional vodka.

3. Vigorously shake the shaker until all ingredients are well mixed.

4. Strain the shaker ingredients into the prepared martini glass.

5. Skewer the sugar-free buckeye candies and place in the glass for garnish.

Chocolate and peanut butter make a delicious Buckeye Smoothie. When you need a buckeye candy fix, you can just drop the ingredients into a blender and let your taste buds do the rest of the work. Make

sure your glass is chilled before you add the chocolate shell. A cold glass will help the chocolate shell set quickly and give you the desired look for your Buckeye Smoothie.

Buckeye Smoothie[40]

Ingredients

1 banana, frozen
3 tablespoons unsweetened cocoa powder
¾ cup vanilla low-fat yogurt
¾ cup milk (more or less to desired texture)
1 tablespoon creamy peanut butter
1 tablespoon honey (more or less to taste)
1 ounce chocolate shell syrup (garnish)
Ice (optional; more or less to desired texture)

Directions

1. Blend the frozen banana and optional ice.

2. Add the cocoa powder and then the liquid ingredients. Add the peanut butter and honey and blend until desired smoothness is reached.

3. Drizzle chocolate shell around the sides of a chilled glass. Once chocolate is set, fill with smoothie mixture and serve.

Preparing the glass properly is the most important part of the Buckeye White Russian recipe. Have enough glasses available for the number of guests you will be serving. If it's just you, prepare an extra glass— you won't regret it. Once you get the rims fully coated with peanut butter, cocoa powder, and salt, you are ready to mix your drinks and serve.

Buckeye White Russian[41]

Ingredients

4 teaspoons peanut butter
3 ounces vodka
2 ounces Kahlúa
2 ounces low-fat milk
Ice cubes
Salt (garnish)
Peanut butter (garnish)
Cocoa powder (garnish)

Directions

1. On a small plate, spread a thick layer of peanut butter, making sure the circumference is larger than your intended serving glasses.

2. On a separate plate, sprinkle salt and cocoa powder, making sure the circumference is larger than your intended serving glasses.

3. Dip each glass in the peanut butter on the plate and then dip the peanut butter–covered rims into the cocoa powder and salt mixture.

4. Place milk, vodka, peanut butter, and Kahlúa in a blender. Blend until peanut butter is thoroughly mixed in.

5. Place two ice cubes in each glass and then pour the blended drink mixture over the cubes in each glass.

Start your day with a Buckeye Latte. What better way to start each midwestern morning than the fresh smell of warm chocolate and peanut butter? This is far from a zero-calorie black coffee, but it sure is much tastier. If you're health conscious or calorie counting, you may want to save this drink for special occasions. But if you're not worried about the points or carbs, why not splurge a little on this fantastic Buckeye Latte?

Buckeye Latte[42]

Ingredients

½ cup hot black coffee
½ cup milk, divided
2 tablespoons powdered peanut butter
½ tablespoon unsweetened cocoa powder
1 teaspoon confectioners' sugar
2 tablespoons Godiva White Chocolate Liqueur
2 tablespoons Kahlúa
Chocolate shavings (garnish)
Whipped cream (garnish)
Buckeye candy (garnish)

Directions

1. Warm up ¼ cup milk.

2. In shaker, combine the warm milk and coffee with powdered peanut butter, cocoa powder, and confectioners' sugar. Shake well.

3. Pour the mixture into a coffee mug and add Kahlúa and Godiva White Chocolate liqueur.

4. Place the remaining ¼ cup milk in a clean shaker. Shake vigorously for 60 seconds until the milk turns into foam. Microwave the foam for up to 45 seconds to help it stabilize.

5. Spoon the foam on top of the coffee.

6. Top the coffee with the whipped cream, chocolate, and buckeye candy.

The Boozy Buckeye is a simple way to get your buckeye fix. Add a little bourbon to some hot chocolate, stir in some peanut butter, and you're ready to drink. If you want to skip a step, you can pick up a fresh cup of hot chocolate at a café or coffee shop on your way home, and you

won't even have to warm the water. This is a great drink for tailgate parties because it only requires some hot water. If the water is hot enough, the peanut butter will melt in the Boozy Buckeye after a few minutes. Take an electric water kettle with you on your next trip, and this drink will be easy to make.

Boozy Buckeye[43]

Ingredients

2 packets hot chocolate mix
1 ½ cups hot water
¼ cup bourbon
1 teaspoon melted peanut butter
Chocolate whipped cream (garnish)
Buckeye candy (garnish)

Directions

1. Stir the hot chocolate packets into the hot water.

2. Add the bourbon to the hot chocolate and stir.

3. Soften the peanut butter in the microwave for 30 seconds and then stir the peanut butter.

4. Top the bourbon and hot chocolate with chocolate whipped cream and a buckeye candy and then drizzle with softened peanut butter.

This drink's name hearkens back to the original use of the term buckeye. The Buck-Eye Cocktail uses the most basic buckeye ingredients— chocolate syrup and peanut butter with a little splash of vodka. Mix all the ingredients together and place them in the prepared glass and you will have a quick and easy buckeye drink—and don't forget to add the buckeye candies.

The Buck-Eye Cocktail[44]

Ingredients

2 ounces vodka
½ ounce peanut butter syrup
½ ounce chocolate syrup
Cocoa powder (garnish)
2 buckeye candies (garnish)

Directions

1. In a bowl, pour a thin layer of water, deep enough to cover the rim of your martini glass.

2. On a separate plate, sprinkle cocoa powder, making sure the circumference is larger than your intended serving glasses.

3. Dip your martini glass in the water and then dip it in the cocoa powder to cover the rim of the glass in a thin coat of chocolate powder.

4. Combine all the ingredients in a shaker and shake vigorously.

5. Pour into martini glass and garnish with a skewer of buckeyes.

This Buckeye Cocktail is for the buckeye connoisseur who wants a little more artistry in their mixed drink. Whipped cream vodka is not a staple on every shelf, so you will have to do some advance purchases to get the ingredients for this drink. But if you put in the preparation and purchase the required ingredients, you will be aptly rewarded with a flavorful Buckeye Cocktail. This recipes requires the Chocolate Shot Glass recipe.

Buckeye Cocktail[45]

Ingredients

2 tablespoons peanut butter

2 tablespoons powdered sugar

1 teaspoon vanilla

1 tablespoon milk

2 ounces whipped cream vodka

½ ounce chocolate-flavored liqueur

Directions

1. Mix the peanut butter, powdered sugar, vanilla, and milk together in a bowl.

2. Microwave the mixture for up to 30 seconds.

3. Scoop 1 tablespoon of the peanut butter mixture into glass.

4. Add vodka and chocolate liqueur and stir.

5. Strain mixture into another container.

6. Pour into chocolate shot glass and serve.

The Chocolate Shot Glass is a versatile addition to any cook's kitchen. It can be used in desserts and for drinks. Be creative about how you use the Chocolate Shot Glass in your recipes. In this book, we are using the Chocolate Shot Glass as an actual container for alcoholic liquids. Once used, the glass can then be eaten as a chaser.

Chocolate Shot Glass[46]

Ingredients

¼ cup dark chocolate

¼ cup milk chocolate

1 Dixie Cup

Directions

1. Melt chocolate in a glass bowl in the microwave in 30-second intervals or in a double boiler over the stove.

2. Take a Dixie Cup and cut a small slit in the top ridge. This will make it easier to peel off the paper later.

3. Coat the inside of the cup with the chocolate mixture.

4. Refrigerate to set for at least 30 minutes.

5. Once the chocolate is set, peel away the paper. Be careful not to break the chocolate.

This slushy can be made with or without alcohol. For the nonalcoholic version, just skip the coconut rum and Kahlúa. The Hard Buckeye Slushy is a twist on the midwestern summer dessert classic slushy. Make sure you don't overblend the ice. If you blend the ice for too long, the heat from some less expensive blenders will begin to melt the ice, which will make your drink too runny.

Hard Buckeye Slushy

Ingredients

2 packets hot chocolate mix
1 ½ cups hot water
¼ cup coconut rum
1 ounce Kahlúa
2 cups ice (more or less to desired thickness)
Whipped cream (garnish)
1 teaspoon peanut butter, melted (garnish)
1 buckeye candy (garnish)

Directions

1. Stir the hot chocolate packets into the hot water.

2. Add the Kahlúa and rum to the hot chocolate and stir.

3. Blend the drink mixture and ice in a blender until well combined.

4. Top with whipped cream and a buckeye candy, then drizzle with melted peanut butter.

The Easy Buckeye Shot is not as easy as it sounds. It consists of only two or three ingredients, but the pouring of those ingredients can be tricky—if you don't have a steady hand. Go slow at first until you get the hang of pouring the alcohol over the spoon. This drink requires perfect layering of the ingredients, but once you get the hang of it, it will make an impressive party addition. If you want to increase the alcohol content, add a small layer of vodka at the top.

Easy Buckeye Shot[47]

Ingredients

¾ ounce Kahlúa
¾ ounce Bailey's Irish Cream
1 spoon
¼ ounce vodka (optional)

Directions

1. Pour the Kahlúa in the bottom of a tall shot glass. Pour the Kahlúa straight down, trying not to get any on the sides of the shot glass.

2. Place the spoon inside the shot glass, upside down. Make sure the tip of the spoon is against the inside edge of the glass. For some liquors, you will need to adjust the height of the spoon above the Kahlúa. Try just above the Kahlúa layer, but you can move it up or down as needed.

3. As slowly as you can, pour the Bailey's Irish Cream over the back of the spoon. Make sure you move the spoon level up as the alcohol rises.

Other Buckeye Recipes

Some recipes don't play nice with others and couldn't fit easily in any category. We have a selection of miscellaneous buckeye recipes that will push you to your chocolatey, peanut-buttery limits. From fudge to dip, there's the perfect little buckeye snack for you or your loved ones. And if you don't like snacks, try buckeyes for breakfast with a stack of buckeye pancakes—you won't regret it!

No party is complete without some kind of dip. Why not make your next party's dip a Buckeye Dip? The Buckeye Dip is a perfect dessert dip for any tailgate, potluck, or family gathering. Be creative with the dippers. You can use the standard graham crackers, pretzels, and apples, but you can also branch out to biscotti, strawberries, Nilla Wafers, or any other unique dip delivery system you can come up with.

Buckeye Dip[48]

Ingredients

8 ounces cream cheese, softened

½ cup butter, softened

1 cup creamy peanut butter

2 cups powdered sugar

3 tablespoons brown sugar

¼ cup all-purpose flour

1 teaspoon vanilla

1 ½ cups mini semisweet chocolate chips

Directions

1. Mix the cream cheese with the butter and peanut butter until smooth. It's best to use a stand mixer, but an electric hand mixer will also work.

2. Add in all the remaining ingredients except for the chocolate chips. Mix until smooth.

3. Fold in the chocolate chips until well mixed.

4. Serve with apples, graham crackers, pretzels, etc.

You can't go too far in the Midwest without finding a local fudge shop. But with this Buckeye Fudge recipe, you don't need to leave the comfort of your own home to get your fudge fix. A proper Buckeye Fudge combines both fudge layers together, but if you are not in a buckeye mood, you can eat each layer independently from the other—you can also use this recipe to make just chocolate or peanut butter fudge.

Buckeye Fudge[49]

Ingredients

PEANUT BUTTER LAYER

1 ¼ cups creamy peanut butter
1 ¼ cups butter, cut into 9 pieces
1 ½ teaspoons vanilla
4 cups powdered sugar

CHOCOLATE LAYER

2 cups semisweet chocolate chips
1 cup sweetened condensed milk
2 ½ tablespoons butter

Directions

1. For peanut butter layer, microwave peanut butter and butter, melting and stirring in 30-second increments until smooth.

2. Add vanilla and gradually whisk in powdered sugar.

3. Pour into a slightly greased 8- or 9-inch square pan.

4. In another bowl, combine and microwave chocolate chips, sweetened condensed milk, and remaining butter, mixing and stirring in 30-second increments until smooth.

5. Pour chocolate mixture on top of peanut butter layer and smooth it out.

6. Chill for 2 hours. Cut into squares to serve.

Being that buckeyes come from a tree, there is no more appropriate name for this dessert than Buckeye Bark. Making Buckeye Bark just requires a series of melting, spreading, and cooling steps. Once everything is cooled and set, you simply break and serve. Breaking Buckeye Bark into pieces is one of the most satisfying ways to serve a dessert.

Buckeye Bark[50]

Ingredients

1 package almond bark
2 cups creamy peanut butter
1 teaspoon vanilla
1 cup powdered sugar

Directions

1. Melt almond bark according to the package directions. Line a baking sheet with parchment paper and pour half of the melted almond bark on top. Spread evenly and freeze for 15 minutes until set.

2. Combine peanut butter, powdered sugar, and vanilla until smooth.

3. Retrieve almond bark from freezer. Spread peanut butter mixture over the almond bark.

4. Coat the peanut butter layer with the remaining almond bark.

5. Return to freezer for 15 minutes until set.

6. Cut or break into pieces to serve.

This recipe is a variation on Buckeye Bark, with the substitution and addition of a few ingredients, most importantly the namesake ingredient, peppermint. Peppermint Buckeye Bark is a great dessert to make for a winter holiday party and even makes a great gift for a

coworker or friend. On those coldest winter days, nothing beats nibbling on a piece of Peppermint Buckeye Bark with your morning coffee.

Peppermint Buckeye Bark[51]

Ingredients

1 cup white chocolate peanut butter
½ cup chunky peanut butter
1 cup powdered sugar
1 teaspoon vanilla
Pinch of salt
3 cups semisweet or bittersweet chocolate, melted
2–3 candy canes, crushed

Directions

1. Melt chocolate according to the package directions. Line a baking sheet with parchment paper and pour half of the melted chocolate on top. Spread evenly and freeze for 15 minutes until set.

2. In a bowl, combine peanut butter, powdered sugar, vanilla, and salt until smooth.

3. Remove the cooled chocolate from the freezer and pour the peanut butter on top. Smooth to make an even layer.

4. Coat the peanut butter layer with the remaining chocolate.

5. Top with the crushed candy canes.

6. Return to freezer for 15 minutes until set.

7. Cut or break into pieces to serve.

We couldn't leave breakfast out of the buckeye candy recipes. These Buckeye Pancakes are sure to please your family and friends, especially if you live in Ohio. Be sure to remember that these Buckeye Pancakes take significantly longer to prepare than regular pancakes, but the extra work has a much higher flavor payoff. I don't think these

will become a staple of every kitchen, but they sure are fun to make for special occasions.

Buckeye Pancakes[52]

Ingredients

BUCKEYE FILLING

¾ cup creamy peanut butter
¼ cup butter, softened
½ teaspoon vanilla
¼ teaspoon salt
1 ½ cups powdered sugar

PANCAKES

2 ¼ cups all-purpose flour
⅔ cup plus 2 tablespoons cocoa powder
¼ cup brown sugar
½ cup sugar
2 tablespoons baking powder
1 ½ teaspoons salt
¼ cup plus 2 tablespoons canola oil
2 large eggs
1 teaspoon vanilla
1 cup brewed coffee, room temperature
1 cup whole milk
½ cup peanut butter
Whipped cream (garnish)
Buckeye candies (garnish)

Directions

1. In a bowl, combine peanut butter, butter, vanilla, and salt until smooth.

2. Gradually mix in powdered sugar until fully incorporated.

3. Roll the peanut butter mixture into 14 equal-sized balls.

4. Line a baking sheet with wax paper. Flatten each ball into a 4-inch disc shape. Chill in freezer for one hour.

5. Heat a greased griddle to 325 degrees Fahrenheit.

6. In a separate bowl, combine flour, cocoa powder, brown sugar, sugar, baking powder, and salt until well combined.

7. Stir in oil, eggs, vanilla, coffee, and milk. Mix until smooth.

8. Pour ¼ cup pancake batter onto the hot griddle and then place one of the peanut butter discs on top. Spoon enough additional batter over the disc to cover completely.

9. Cook pancake until the edges begin to bubble.

10. Flip pancake and cook for an additional 2 minutes or until cooked through.

11. Microwave ½ cup peanut butter for 30-second increments until it is drizzling consistency. Drizzle over the buckeye pancakes and then top with whipped cream and buckeyes.

These Vegan Buckeye Pancakes allow you to have the thrill of eating buckeye-flavored pancakes without any additions of eggs. Make sure you start your recipe by preparing the flax egg substitute, and don't forget to pick up some of your favorite vegan dark chocolate.

Vegan Buckeye Pancakes[53]

Ingredients

FLAX EGG
1 tablespoon flaxseed meal
2 tablespoons water

PANCAKES

1 tablespoon coconut oil, melted

½ teaspoon vanilla

¾–1 cup unsweetened vanilla almond milk

2–3 tablespoons agave nectar

1 teaspoon baking powder

½ teaspoon baking soda

1 ½ tablespoons natural salted creamy peanut butter

Pinch of salt

½ cup finely ground oat flour

¼ cup whole wheat

2 tablespoons unsweetened dark cocoa powder

Buckeye candies (garnish)

SYRUP

¼ cup agave nectar

2 tablespoons natural salted creamy peanut butter

⅛ teaspoon vanilla

4 mini vegan dark chocolate peanut butter cups,
   cut into fourths

Directions

1. In a small bowl, combine flaxseed meal with water to make a flax egg.

2. Preheat griddle to medium heat or 350 degrees Fahrenheit.

3. In a bowl combine flax egg, coconut oil, agave nectar, baking soda, baking powder, salt, and vanilla until smooth. Gradually add almond milk until fully incorporated.

4. Stir in oat flour and whole wheat until well mixed.

5. Divide batter evenly between two bowls.

6. In one bowl, add cocoa powder until combined.

7. In the other bowl, add peanut butter until combined.

8. On a hot griddle, pour ¼ cup of chocolate batter, then immediately pour ¼ cup of peanut butter batter in the center of the chocolate batter. Cook until bubbles form and then flip and cook for an additional 2 minutes.

9. For the syrup, combine agave, peanut butter, and vanilla. Microwave and stir in 30-second increments until smooth and runny.

10. Stack 3–4 pancakes and pour syrup over the top. Place 1–2 buckeyes on top.

Buckeye Cream Puffs require a little bit of baking prowess, but even an average baker should be able to make these delicious cream puffs in their own kitchen. It is important to follow the directions. Make sure you rotate the pans and lower the temperature of the oven. If you forget, you will have lopsided and burnt clamshells instead of cream puffs.

Buckeye Cream Puffs[54]

Ingredients

1 cup water
8 tablespoons unsalted butter
¼ teaspoon salt
1 ¼ cups all-purpose flour
4 large eggs
¼ cup peanut butter
½ cup powdered sugar
½ teaspoon vanilla
⅛ teaspoon salt
2 cups heavy whipping cream
1 ¼ cups bittersweet chocolate chips (garnish)
¾ cup heavy whipping cream (garnish)

Directions

1. Preheat oven to 425 degrees Fahrenheit.

2. Line two pans with parchment paper.

3. Melt butter on the stove butter. Mix in water and salt and stir until it boils.

4. Remove from heat and add flour. Stir until dough is smooth.

5. After mixture cools, add eggs, one at a time, until well mixed.

6. Divide dough into six equal portions and place on pans.

7. Bake for 15 minutes.

8. Rotate the pans in the oven and lower the temperature to 350 degrees Fahrenheit.

9. Bake for another 25 minutes at 350 degrees Fahrenheit.

10. While cream puffs cool, whisk together the peanut butter, powdered sugar, vanilla, cream, and salt.

11. Whip the mixture into a cream.

12. Pull apart the top and bottom of cream puffs and stuff with the peanut butter cream.

13. Heat the remaining heavy cream in a microwave for 2 minutes. Once heated, pour the cream over a bowl of chocolate chips.

14. Let the mixture sit for 1 minute before folding the chocolate and cream together. Stir until smooth.

15. Using a spoon, drizzle the chocolate cream mixture over the cream puffs.

These Buckeye Graham Crackers are delicious on their own, but they also make a perfect dipper for the Buckeye Dip recipe. You can crumble these Buckeye Graham Crackers to make a pie crust for Buckeye Pie, or you can add a new twist to buckeye s'mores. Be creative and don't limit yourself with these crackers.

Buckeye Graham Crackers[55]

Ingredients

1 ½ cups creamy peanut butter
½ cup butter, softened
2 ½ cups powdered sugar
12 graham crackers
3 cups semisweet chocolate chips
2 tablespoons coconut oil
½ cup peanut butter chips (garnish)
1 teaspoon coconut oil (garnish)

Directions

1. Line pans with parchment paper.

2. In a large bowl, combine peanut butter, powdered sugar, and butter until fully incorporated.

3. Roll dough into roughly 1-inch balls.

4. Place each doughball on a half graham cracker. Press it flat and be careful not to break the graham cracker.

5. Line the pans with the crackers.

6. Melt the chocolate and coconut oil.

7. Use tongs to dip each cracker, peanut butter facing down, into the chocolate. Coat the peanut butter and sides of the cracker, but be careful not to coat the graham cracker.

8. Return crackers to parchment.

9. In another saucepan, melt peanut butter and coconut oil.

10. Drizzle peanut butter mixture over the chocolate layer of the graham crackers.

11. Allow to set at room temperature for 30–60 minutes.

On those hot midwestern summer days, nothing beats kicking back in a lawn chair with a bowl full of Buckeye Fudge Ice Cream. You can also scoop up this ice cream and serve it in cones or add it to a Buckeye Smoothie for an extra blast of buckeye goodness. No matter how you eat Buckeye Fudge Ice Cream, you'll be delighted every time.

Buckeye Fudge Ice Cream[56]

Ingredients

2 cups heavy cream, divided
14 ounces sweetened condensed milk
¾ cup unsweetened cocoa powder
1 tablespoon vanilla
¾ cup semisweet chocolate chips
Pinch of flaky sea salt
½ cup creamy peanut butter
2 tablespoons butter, softened
1–2 cups powdered sugar

Directions

1. Whisk together 1 cup heavy cream, sweetened condensed milk, cocoa powder, and vanilla. Combine until stiff peaks form.

2. In a microwave-safe bowl, combine the remaining 1 cup heavy cream and the chocolate chips. Stir after 30-second intervals in microwave.

3. When chocolate is melted, mix in salt.

4. In a separate bowl, combine peanut butter, butter, and powdered sugar until fully incorporated.

5. Roll peanut butter mixture into marble-size balls.

6. Gently fold peanut butter balls into the chocolate ice cream mixture and place in a freezer-safe container.

7. Freeze 4–6 hours and then serve.

I saved the easiest recipe for last. The Buckeye Shake only has one direction—throw everything into a blender and push the button. It doesn't get much easier than that. You can substitute most of the health-conscious ingredients below with your preferred choices. Just make sure to keep an adequate balance between dry and liquid ingredients so your Buckeye Shake has the proper consistency.

Buckeye Shake

Ingredients

2 scoops low-carb chocolate protein powder
6 ounces almond milk or macadamia nut milk
1 ½ tablespoons peanut butter
1 tablespoon cocoa powder
1 tablespoon cacao nibs (optional)
4 ounces water (more or less for desired thickness)
Crushed ice

Directions

1. Place all ingredients in a blender and blend to desired consistency.

appendix:

The Original Ohio Buckeye Candy Trail

In 2018, the Miami County Visitors and Convention Bureau and Ohio Tourism partnered to create the Ohio Buckeye Candy Trail. They chose to include stores that are still making buckeye candies the traditional way—by hand.

The original Ohio buckeye candy trail stores are all listed here for your ease of reference. Make sure to visit each one when you are in the area. Trust me—they all taste different. From the time-tested chocolates of Winans to the cookie dough buckeyes of Jack-B's, you're sure to find something that will tickle your taste buds.

1. Haute Chocolate

Haute Chocolate is located in the heart of Montgomery. They have been creating freestyle chocolate treats since 1979.

9424 Shelly Lane
Cincinnati, OH 45242
513-793-9999
https://www.haute-chocolate.com/

2. Golden Turtle Chocolate Factory

At Golden Turtle Chocolate Factory, premium chocolates have been prepared by master candymakers since 1982. Their chocolate temptations will satisfy the most discriminating tastes.

120 S. Broadway Street, #1
Lebanon, OH 45036
513-932-1990
http://goldenturtlechocolatefactory.com/

3. Holly B's Sweets

Located in the picturesque antique village of Waynesville, Holly B's Sweets is a family-owned business that takes pride in creating delicious, quality handmade chocolates and fudge.

33 S. Main Street
Waynesville, OH 45068
513-897-2112
https://www.facebook.com/hollybsweets/

4. Friesinger's Chocolates

Friesinger's is a family-owned business that manufactures the finest-quality nuts and candy in two facilities in Dayton and Springboro.

45 N. Pioneer Boulevard
Springboro, OH 45066
937-743-4377
http://www.candyandnutstore.com/

5. Esther Price Candies

As distinctive as Esther Price's gold box, so is the taste of their chocolates. Esther Price Candies continues the tradition of old-fashioned quality using the same recipes that Esther Price herself perfected since 1926!

1709 Wayne Avenue
Dayton, OH 45410
800-782-0326
http://www.estherprice.com/

6. Winans Chocolates + Coffees

Established in the early 1900s and located in the quaint, historic setting of downtown Piqua, Winans creates premium chocolates, handmade the same way for generations.

310 Spring Street
Piqua, OH 45356
937-773-1981
http://winanschocolatesandcoffees.com/

7. Marie's Candies

Marie's Candies opened its doors in 1956, and its reputation for old-fashioned, high-quality candies spread across the countryside.

311 Zanesfield Road
West Liberty, OH 43357
937-465-3061
https://mariescandies.com/

8. Jack-B's

Jack-B's is at your service with home-cooked goodness-to-go including their Peanut Butter or Cookie Dough Buckeyes dipped in white or milk chocolate.

124 E. Sandusky Street
Findlay, OH 45840
567-294-4234
https://jackbsfindlay.com/

8. Dietsch Brothers Fine Chocolates & Ice Cream

In 1937, Dietsch Brothers began producing fine chocolates and ice cream using original family recipes and have been producing delicious, quality products ever since.

400 W. Main Cross Street
Findlay, OH 45840
419-422-4474
https://dietschs.com/

10. Marsha's Homemade Buckeyes

For more than thirty years Marsha's has specialized in manufacturing peanut butter and chocolate candy buckeyes. The buckeye is the only candy that they make, so their goal has always been to produce the perfect one.

25631 Ft. Meigs Road, Suite H
Perrysburg, OH 43551
419-872-7666
https://marshasbuckeyes.com/

11. Sweet Tooth Cottage

Sweet Tooth Cottage is a family-owned bakery in Powell, Ohio. Everything they sell is made by hand and from scratch in their kitchen.

10221 Sawmill Parkway
Powell, OH 43065
614-361-6166
http://www.sweettoothcottage.com/

12. Eagle Family Candy

Operating in the same location and with the original equipment and recipes, Eagle Family Candy takes pride in making quality, local, delicious chocolates.

4590 N. High Street
Columbus, OH 43214
614-262-2255
https://www.eaglefamilycandy.com/

13. Tremont Goodie Shop

The Tremont Goodie Shop is a full-line, family-owned bakery nestled in Upper Arlington, Ohio. For more than sixty years, they've handmade their products from scratch and served their customers—who are more like friends—with a smile.

2116 Tremont Center
Upper Arlington, OH 43221
614-488-8777
http://www.theoriginalgoodieshop.com/

14. Anthony Thomas

Anthony Thomas is one of the largest family-owned-and-operated candy companies in the Midwest. They produce an average of fifty thousand pounds of chocolates daily.

1777 Arlingate Lane
Columbus, OH 43228
877-226-3921
https://www.anthony-thomas.com/

15. Chocolate Café

Serving the area since 2007, at the Chocolate Café, you can order your hand-rolled buckeyes to go in an edible chocolate box.

1855 Northwest Boulevard
Columbus, OH 43212
614-485-2233
https://www.chocolatecafecolumbus.com/

16. Pure Imagination Chocolatier

Pure Imagination Chocolatier was founded by Master Chocolatier Daniel Cooper in 2001. It has been awarded the finest chocolate in Columbus since 2002.

1205 Grandview Avenue
Grandview Heights, OH 43212
614-488-3070
http://pureimaginationchocolatier.com/

17. Schmidt's Fudge Haus

At Schmidt's Fudge Haus, they only offer the finest fudge and chocolates made with the finest ingredients. Their buckeyes will make you scream OH-IO!

220 E. Kossuth Street
Columbus, OH 43206
614-444-2222
http://www.schmidtsfudgehaus.com/

18. Wittich's Candy Shop

Celebrating 178 years in business, Wittich's Candy Shop is the nation's oldest family-owned-and-operated candy shop. Try one of their buckeyes in the Buckeye Blast Sundae: Smith's Buckeye Blast ice cream topped with chocolate and peanut butter sauce, real whipped cream, and a Wittich buckeye.

117 W. High Street
Circleville, OH 43113
740-474-3313
http://wittichscandyshop.com/

19. Buckeye Creations

Buckeye Creations offers the classic Ohio candy with a unique and creative twist of flavors. From coconut to s'mores, each one has its own personality and unique taste.

6962 Willow Bloom Drive
Canal Winchester, OH 43110
614-209-1617
https://www.facebook.com/BuckeyeCreations/

20. Candy Cottage

The Candy Cottage is a locally owned confectionery, and their legacy dates back to the 1960s. They specialize in unique holiday treats, custom favors for any occasion, baskets, corporate gifts, chocolate boxes, and more.

2271 W. Fair Avenue
Lancaster, OH 43130
740-653-6842
http://candycottageltd.com/

21. Goumas Candyland

It's always buckeye season at Goumas Candyland, and people can't get enough. Aside from using only the best ingredients, the secret lies in traditional recipes, passed down through the generations.

19 Claren Drive
Heath, OH 43056
740-345-7440
https://goumascandyland.com/

22. Nothing But Chocolate

Nothing But Chocolate is a chocolate business located in historic Cambridge, Ohio. Their most popular item is an Ohio tradition. Each box of buckeyes is made to order to ensure delicious fresh buckeyes dipped for you.

731 Wheeling Avenue
Cambridge, OH 43725
740-439-5754
https://www.nothingbutchocolate.com/

23. Coblentz Chocolates

Coblentz Chocolate Company began in 1987 and is nestled in Ohio's Amish country. They hold true to the local traditions of doing things the old-fashioned way. They use the freshest ingredients.

4917 State Route 515
Walnut Creek, OH 44687
800-338-9341
https://coblentzchocolates.com/

24. Sweeties Chocolates at Grandpa's Cheesebarn

With more than forty years in the business, they continue to welcome visitors from all over the globe to savor the experience of their sweet dream come true.

668 US Highway 250 E.
Ashland, OH 44085
419-281-3202
https://grandpascheesebarn.com/

25. Waggoner Chocolates

At Waggoner Chocolates, they continue their timeless devotion to the world's most distinguished chocolate connoisseurs by providing quality chocolates and confections that will be cherished for generations to come.

1281 S. Main Street
North Canton, OH 44720
330-433-1834
https://www.waggonerchocolates.com/

26. Harry London Candies

For nearly a century, Fannie May Chocolates has been bringing their customers the finest gourmet chocolates, fudge, and candies that have kept them as a favorite traditional chocolate store.

5353 Lauby Road
North Canton, OH 44720
800-999-3629
https://www.fanniemay.com/store/harry-london/

27. Honadle's Fine Chocolates at Hartville Kitchen

Just like the corner candy store you remember as a child, their candy shop features creamy homemade fudge and a variety of hand-dipped chocolates to satisfy your sweet tooth.

1015 Edison Street NW
Hartville, OH 44632
330-877-9353
http://www.hartvillekitchen.com/candy-shop/chocolates/

28. Butter Maid Bakery

Family owned and operated since 1955, they make old-fashioned handmade products in small batches.

425 Boardman Canfield Road
Boardman, OH 44512
844-688-7655
https://www.buttermaidbakery.com/

29. Malley's Chocolates

Now in the third generation of family business, Malley's Chocolates is committed to offering quality confections made with the same special-recipe milk and dark chocolate they've earned their stellar reputation providing.

1685 Victoria Avenue
Lakewood, OH 44107
216-226-8300
https://malleys.com/

30. Campbell's Sweets Factory

The heritage at Campbell's Sweets began more than four decades ago in the roots of candy making excellence. Campbell's feels good about getting behind all their products with the quality of ingredients they use!

2084 W. 25th Street
Cleveland, OH 44113
216-965-0451
https://campbellssweets.com/

31. Buckeye Chocolate Company

In its second generation, the Buckeye Chocolate Company is devoted to providing customers with fresh and quality confections.

510 Water Street
Chardon, OH 44024
440-286-5282
https://www.buckeyechocolate.com/

Off the Trail

Buckeye Donuts
1998 N. High Street, Columbus, OH 43201

Whit's Frozen Custard
3339 N. High Street, Columbus, OH 43202

Graeter's Ice Cream
1534 W. Lane Avenue, Columbus, OH 43221

notes

3. People, Places, and Things (and the Buckeye Candy)

1. T. F. Thiselton-Dyer, *The Folk-lore of Plants* (New York: Mythik Press, 2015), 177.

2. Gerina Dunwich, *Herbal Magick: A Witch's Guide to Herbal Enchantments, Folklore, and Divination* (New York: Weiser, 2008), 72.

4. The Original Buckeye Recipe

1. Guy Lucas, "The Origin of Buckeye Balls," *Newsroom with a View: Thoughts from One Journalist*, June 10, 2012, https://guylucas .com/2012/06/10/the-origin-of-buckeye-balls/.

2. Brian Lewis, "The Side Effects of Paraffin Wax," Leaftv: Feel Good, accessed February 11, 2020, https://www.leaf.tv/5847488/the -side-effects-of-paraffin-wax/.

3. "Paraffin Poisoning," MedlinePlus, last updated October 11, 2018, https://medlineplus.gov/ency/article/002731.htm.

5. Recipes

1. The Gold Lining Girl, "Potato Chip White Chocolate Buckeyes Recipe," But First, Dessert! (blog), January 16, 2018, https://thegold lininggirl.com/2018/01/potato-chip-white-chocolate-buckeyes -recipe/?utm_source=newsletter&utm_medium=email&utm _campaign=potato_chip_white_chocolate_buckeyes_recipe&utm _term=2018-01-17.

2. "Bourbon Buckeyes with a Surprise—Traditional Buckeyes," Take Two Tapas (blog), November 20, 2019, https://www.taketwo tapas.com/bourbon-buckeyes-with-a-surprise-inside-2/.

3. "Healthy Buckeye Balls," Desserts with Benefits (blog), January 12, 2017, https://dessertswithbenefits.com/ healthy-buckeye-balls/.

4. Paula Miller, "The Best Ever Almond Buckeyes," Recipes, Whole Intentions, last updated October 19, 2018, https://wholeintentions.com/best-ever-almond-butter-buckeyes/.

5. "Keto Buckeyes Chocolate and Peanut Butter Balls Recipe," iSave A to Z, December 2, 2017, https://www.isavea2z.com/keto-buckeyes-chocolate-peanut-butter-balls-recipe/.

6. "The Best Paleo Buckeyes," Living Well Mom, December 9, 2015, https://livingwellmom.com/best-paleo-buckeyes/.

7. "Sugar-Free Low Carb Buckeyes," Low Carb Diet World, November 14, 2018, https://lowcarbdietworld.com/sugar-free-low-carb-buckeyes/.

8. Erin Alderson, "Peanut Butter Buckeyes with Popped Quinoa," Ancient Harvest, accessed February 11, 2020, https://ancientharvest.com/recipe-items/peanut-butter-buckeye-with-popped-quinoa/.

9. Miss Bosslady, "Cookie Butter Buckeye Candies," Mind over Batter (blog), January 26, 2017, http://www.mind-over-batter.com/brownies-bars/cookie-butter-buckeye-candies/#wprm-recipe-container-14724.

10. Haley, "Buckeye Cake Pops," Flour Covered Apron (blog), October 26, 2017, https://flourcoveredapron.com/buckeye-cake-pops/.

11. "Crunchy Kahlúa Buckeyes with Sea Salt," Hungry Couple (blog), December 4, 2013, https://www.hungrycouplenyc.com/2013/12/edible-gifts-crunchy-kahlua-buckeyes.html?m=1.

12. Alisa, "Gingerbread Almond Butter Buckeyes," Paleo in PDX (blog), accessed February 11, 2020, http://paleoinpdx.com/2018/12/10/gingerbread-almond-butter-buckeyes/.

13. Lindsay Grimes Freeman, "Banana Bread Buckeyes," The Toasted Pine Nut (blog), January 18, 2017, https://thetoastedpinenut.com/banana-bread-buckeyes/.

14. Jess Larson, "Tahini Buckeyes," Plays Well with Butter: Everyday Recipes for Modern Gals (blog), accessed February 11, 2020, https://playswellwithbutter.com/2018/12/04/tahini-buckeye-cookies/.

15. Tieghan Gerard, "Healthy Harvest Buckeyes," Half Baked Harvest (blog), September 16, 2014, https://www.halfbakedharvest.com/healthy-harvest-buckeyes/.

16. This recipe was created by Carolyn Nespeca and provided by Kellie Brokway, her daughter.

17. Lizzy T, "Cookie Dough Buckeyes," Tastes of Lizzy T (blog), September 14, 2016, https://www.tastesoflizzyt.com/cookie-dough-buckeyes/#wprm-recipe-container-17333.

18. Ashton Epps Swank, "Cookie Dough Buckeyes," Something Swanky (blog), March 24, 2014, https://www.somethingswanky.com/cookie-dough-buckeyes/.

19. Elizabeth LaBau, "Homemade Crunchy Buckeyes Candy," The Spruce Eats, last updated October 20, 2019, https://www.thespruce eats.com/crunchy-buckeyes-521165.

20. Shell, "Buckeye Pretzels," Things I Can't Say: Tips and Tales from an Introverted Mom (blog), http://thingsicantsay.com/buckeye -pretzels/.

21. Erica and Abe, "Buckeye Crunch Bars," The Crumby Kitchen: Crave-Worthy Cooking Despite the Crumbs (blog), September 17, 2015, https://thecrumbykitchen.com/buckeye-crunch-bars/.

22. Michelle Palin, "Gluten-Free Buckeye Brownies," My Gluten-Free Kitchen (blog), November 15, 2019, https://mygluten -freekitchen.com/buckeye-brownies-gluten-free/?utm_medium =social&utm _source=pinterest&utm_campaign=tailwind_tribes&utm_content =tribes&utm_term=368756400_11891078_334819.

23. Kelly Smith, "Healthy Buckeye Bars," So Much to Make (blog), February 23, 2016, http://www.somuchtomake.com/2016/02/healthy -buckeye-bars.html.

24. Erin, "Buckeye Bundt Cake," The Spiffy Cookie (blog), October 14, 2017, https://www.thespiffycookie.com/2017/10/14/buckeye -bundt-cake/.

25. Kim, "'Awesome' Peanut Butter Buckeye Rice Krispies," The Baking ChocolaTess (blog), July 6, 2015, https://www.thebaking chocolatess.com/awesome-peanut-butter-buckeye-rice-krispies/.

26. Melissa, "Buckeye Turtle Brownies," MamaGourmand: How a Foodie Feeds a Family (blog), January 24, 2017, last updated March 31, 2019, https://www.mamagourmand.com/buckeye-turtle -brownies/.

27. Lena Abraham, "Buckeye Pie," Delish, July 11, 2018, https:// www.delish.com/cooking/recipe-ideas/recipes/a56618/buckeye-pie -recipe/.

28. Carlee, "Buckeye Cheesecake with a Brownie Crust," Cooking with Carlee: A Collection of Family Favorite Recipes Both Old and New (blog), August 15, 2018, https://www.cookingwithcarlee.com /2018/08/buckeye-cheesecake-with-brownie-crust.html.

29. Lisa Huff, "Mini Buckeye Cheesecakes," Snappy Gourmet (blog), November 21, 2019, https://snappygourmet.com/mini -buckeye-cheesecakes/.

30. Lindsay, "Buckeye Bars," Veggie Balance (blog), August 9, 2019, https://www.veggiebalance.com/easy-no-bake-peanut-butter -buckeye-bars-recipe/.

31. Lindsay, "Buckeye Bars," Veggie Balance (blog), August 9, 2019, https://www.veggiebalance.com/easy-no-bake-peanut-butter -buckeye-bars-recipe/.

32. Betsy, "Buckeye Brownies," JavaCupCake (blog), August 6, 2013, https://javacupcake.com/2013/08/buckeye-brownies/.

33. Shelly Jaronsky, "Buckeye Brownie Cookies," Cookies & Cups (blog), March 28, 2013, https://cookiesandcups.com/buckeye-brownie-cookies/.

34. Miranda, "Buckeye Thumbprint Cookies," Cookie Dough and Oven Mitt (blog), November 10, 2017, https://www.cookiedough andovenmitt.com/buckeye-thumbprint-cookies/.

35. Erin, "Buckeye Stuffed Chocolate Peanut Butter Cookie Cake," The Spiffy Cookie (blog), November 26, 2016, http://www.the spiffycookie.com/2016/11/26/buckeye-stuffed-chocolate-peanut-butter-cookie-cake/?utm_source=feedburner&utm_medium=email&utm_campaign=Feed:+TheSpiffyCookie+(The+Spiffy+Cookie).

36. Tieghan Gerard, "Ultimate Triple Layer Chocolate Bourbon Peanut Butter Buckeye Cake," Half Baked Harvest (blog), September 13, 2013, https://www.halfbakedharvest.com/ultimate-triple-layer-chocolate-bourbon-peanut-butter-buckeye-cake/.

37. "Peanut Butter Cup Martini," Liquor, accessed February 11, 2020, https://www.liquor.com/recipes/peanut-butter-cup-martini/?utm_campaign=yummly&utm_medium=yummly&utm_source=yummly.

38. Whitney Bond, "Reese's Peanut Butter Cup Martini," Whitney Bond (blog), October 29, 2015, https://whitneybond.com/reeses-peanut-butter-cup-martini/.

39. Denise, "Halloween Low Carb Candy Drinks," My Life Cookbook (blog), October 18, 2017, https://mylifecookbook.com/halloween-low-carb-candy-drinks/?utm_campaign=yummly&utm_medium=yummly&utm_source=yummly.

40. Charlene Maugeri, "'Buckeye' Smoothie with Jif and Dannon," Enduring All Things (blog), May 4, 2016, https://www.enduringall things.com/2016/05/buckeye-smoothie-with-jif-and-dannon.html.

41. "Mini Peanut Butter White Russians," Yummly Peanut Board, accessed February 11, 2020, https://www.yummly.com/recipe/Mini-Peanut-Butter-White-Russians-2435852#print.

42. Linda Warren, "Decadent Buckeye Latte Cocktail," 2 Cookin' Mamas (blog), December 24, 2017, https://2cookinmamas.com/buckeye-latte/.

43. Candace Braun Davison, "The Boozy Buckeye Cocktail Recipe," Delish, August 25, 2015, https://www.delish.com/cooking/recipe-ideas/recipes/a43636/tailgate-cocktail-recipes-ohio-state-boozy-buckeye-recipe/.

44. Marcy Franklin, "The Peanut Butter Buckeye Cocktail," The Daily Meal, November 5, 2012, https://www.thedailymeal.com/recipes/peanut-butter-buck-eye-cocktail-recipe.

45. Adapted from Kitchen Instruments, "How to Make a Buckeye Shot! (Peanut Butter Cup Drink Dessert) | Kitchen Instruments," video, 5:04, September 27, 2018, https://www.youtube.com/watch?v=Z8XssDgfGfk&feature=share.

46. Adapted from Kitchen Instruments, "How to Make SIMPLE Chocolate Shot Glasses for Parties! (Chocolate Recipes) | Kitchen Instruments," video, 1:14, September 25, 2018, https://www.youtube.com/watch?v=07IOIrmbyT4.

47. "Buckeye," ShotStacker, accessed February 11, 2020, https://www.shotstacker.com/drink-recipe-details.php?photo_id=2.

48. Molly, "Buckeye Dip," What Molly Made (blog), December 10, 2015, https://whatmollymade.com/buckeye-dip/#_a5y_p=4493907.

49. Christin Mahrlig, "Buckeye Fudge," Spicy Southern Kitchen (blog), December 12, 2014, https://spicysouthernkitchen.com/buckeye-fudge/.

50. Gail Dickinson, "Buckeye Bark," Chocolate, Chocolate, and More (blog), November 25, 2013, https://chocolatechocolateandmore.com/buckeye-bark/.

51. Susan Palmer, "Buckeye Peppermint Bark," Girl in the Little Red Kitchen (blog), December 11, 2014, http://girlinthelittleredkitchen.com/2014/12/buckeye-peppermint-bark/#_a5y_p=3049971.

52. Julia Clark, "Chocolate Peanut Butter Pancakes (Buckeye Pancakes)," Tastes of Lizzy T (blog), October 26, 2017, https://www.tastesoflizzyt.com/chocolate-peanut-butter-pancakes-buckeye-pancakes-recipe/.

53. Erin, "Vegan Buckeye Pancakes with Peanut Butter Syrup," The Spiffy Cookie (blog), September 14, 2013, http://www.thespiffycookie.com/2013/09/14/vegan-buckeye-pancakes-with-peanut-butter-syrup/.

54. Jill, "Buckeye Cream Puffs," Foodtastic Mom: Cooking Is My Superpower (blog), December 22, 2016, https://www.foodtasticmom.com/buckeye-cream-puffs/.

55. The Gold Lining Girl, "Buckeye Graham Crackers," But First, Dessert! (blog), January 26, 2015, https://thegoldlininggirl.com/2015/01/buckeye-graham-crackers/.

56. Tieghan Gerard, "Buckeye Fudge Ice Cream," Half Baked Harvest (blog), September 2, 2016, https://www.halfbakedharvest.com/buckeye-fudge-ice-cream/.

An award-winning author, CYLE YOUNG loves to write while he sits beside the Grand River. He is passionate about training writers through his online writing academy and at his international writing conferences offered through his company, Serious Writer. He is the author of *Michigan Motivations: A Year of Inspiration with the University of Michigan Wolverines* and numerous children's books. You can find out more about Cyle at his website, www.cyleyoung.com.